Pitman
Education
Library

Gifted Children and the
MILLFIELD EXPERIMENT

If found please return to the College in Oxford

Gifted Children and the MILLFIELD EXPERIMENT

S. A. Bridges
M.A., B.Sc., Ph.D.

Pitman Publishing

First published 1975

Sir Isaac Pitman and Sons Ltd
Pitman House, Parker Street, Kingsway, London WC2B 5PB
PO Box 46038, Banda Street, Nairobi, Kenya

Pitman Publishing Pty Ltd
Pitman House, Bouverie Street, Carlton, Victoria 3053, Australia

Pitman Publishing Corporation
6 East 43rd Street, New York, NY 10017, USA

Sir Isaac Pitman (Canada) Ltd
495 Wellington Street West, Toronto 135, Canada

The Copp Clark Publishing Company
517 Wellington Street West, Toronto 135, Canada

Cased edition ISBN: 0 273 00736 X
Paperback edition ISBN: 0 273 00737 8

Text set in 10/11 IBM Journal Roman, printed by photolithography,
and bound in Great Britain at The Pitman Press, Bath

(G4595/4596:15)

Preface

The book *Gifted Children and the Brentwood Experiment* (Pitman, 1969) was published partly because the team at Brentwood believed that some of the tentative findings were worth reporting and partly in self-defence, as the number of students from other Colleges of Education making inquiries about the work was increasing alarmingly. The book thus served two purposes but it also marked the breaking-up of the experimental team, mainly through promotions and retirements.

When the Headmaster of Millfield, Mr R. J. O. Meyer, knew definitely of the retirement of the author he offered facilities for him to continue his experimental work at Millfield and at the lower school, Edgarley. This book is the outcome of that offer.

One advantage of undertaking such work at Millfield was the availability of a considerable number of children who were gifted on one criterion or another. Moreover, although the fees for the school were very high, many gifted children had been admitted on scholarships (in some cases on nominal fees) so that one was not restricted to working with children from relatively well-off families. Furthermore, the two schools covered the full range of ability to be found in any good Local Education Authority school. A second advantage was that the school was prepared to pay for a certain amount of the materials required. A third advantage was the active support of the Headmasters, Mr Meyer and subsequently Mr C. Atkinson at Millfield, and Mr B. Rushton at Edgarley.

There were also, however, some disadvantages. The first of these was finding a place on the timetable at Millfield for a group which cut across the normal academic groupings. This meant in one case a meeting of the group after games on a sports afternoon and in another a clash with an "O" level subject which deprived the group of three or four of the most interesting children. A second disadvantage was the age of the children who were from 10 to 14 years old. The Brentwood Experiment had demonstrated the need to help children as early as possible in life, preferably not later than 5 or 6 years of age. On the other hand some of the experimental work described below could not have been undertaken with much younger children. A third disadvantage lay in the degree of specialization in subject teaching in both schools. This did mean a relatively small use of the ordinary academic material; however, this did compel the pursuit of other ideas which are at least as important as many academic ideas.

This book is a report on a variety of activities with different groups. As there have always been more children available at Edgarley, and as at Edgarley the groups have met in normal lesson periods, the reports are increasingly based on Edgarley. Some excerpts from the children's work are included so that the reader may form his own conclusions. The chapter entitled "Conclusions" is itself tentative in nature. As in the case of the work at Brentwood it is hoped that some of the techniques described and some of the approaches made to the problems of Gifted Children may be applicable to all the children in our schools.

Acknowledgements

Thanks are due to:

Mr R. J. O. Meyer, OBE, Founder and former Headmaster of Millfield, who made the experimental work possible.

Mr C. R. M. Atkinson, the present Headmaster of Millfield, for permission to publish the report on work done in his school.

Mr B. H. Rushton, Headmaster at Edgarley, for active help and unstinted encouragement.

Mr A. Sparrow, for his liaison work at Millfield and for participation in the programme.

Other members of the teaching staff at Millfield and Edgarley for their help and interest.

The late Mr D. Moir, Primary School Headmaster, for his friendship, help and encouragement.

Mr N. V. King, Careers Master, Mr F. H. Edwards, and Mr N. Grainger, for "volunteering" to talk to the groups.

All the Queer Kids who took part, for their stimulation and toleration.

Mrs M. Nunns, for typing and improving the text as well as providing helpful criticism.

This book is dedicated
to the memory of Duncan Moir

Contents

1

Choosing and Meeting the Groups

Since the experimental work was undertaken in a public school about which several erroneous ideas exist, it would probably be helpful to the reader to have some facts about the school. One persistent, false belief is that Millfield is a school for exceptionally gifted children, usually from wealthy families. In fact there are many gifted children on the roll but the full range of ability is represented and there is a highly developed and efficient remedial department.

Millfield was founded in 1935 by Mr R. J. O. Meyer in a country house at Street in Somerset with a handful of pupils. From this small beginning there has been an enormous development so that now under Mr C. R. M. Atkinson, who succeeded Mr Meyer as Headmaster in 1971, there are over a thousand boys and girls at Millfield and another 250 children at Edgarley Hall, which became the Junior School in 1945, and is now under Mr B. H. Rushton as Headmaster. The majority of the pupils are boarders who live in a number of houses within a few miles of the two schools.

From the outset there were two fundamental policies which have continued to dominate the planning and development of the schools. The first of these has been the encouragement of all forms of ability, whether academic, artistic or athletic. Indeed many people know of Millfield because of the number of tennis or rugby players who have been trained there. Scholarships and bursaries have been readily available for children showing a high potential in a variety of fields. Nevertheless a balance has always been maintained in the entry so that children of all levels of ability have been able to mix. As the Senior

School grew there was a growing demand for facilities for younger members of families and it was this demand which led to the founding of Edgarley, which has also had a wide range of abilities. Most of the children from Edgarley go on to Millfield and this has proved beneficial for many primary school children who have tended to outstrip the provision possible in a number of primary schools both in the public and the private sector of education. Children of high academic ability have been recommended to Edgarley by education authority psychologists and have been accepted often on very generous terms. In other cases parents on discovering that they are facing problems because of the abilities of their children have approached Millfield and Edgarley for help.

The second policy has been that of working on a high teacher-pupil ratio. Usually no child need ever find himself in a group larger than twelve. Many of the groups are smaller and at least in the upper stages of the Senior School it is often possible for pupils to draw up largely personal timetables. Despite the dangers that may arise when one teacher has a higher repuation for pleasantness, efficiency or examination successes than some of his colleagues the system seems to have worked well wherever the pupils have been in earnest. Another advantage of the high teacher-pupil ratio has been the vast number of subjects available, really a necessity in a school which has catered often for more than forty nationalities at one time. For example, in recent years the number of modern languages taught has varied between twenty and thirty. The out-of-school activities are at least as numerous as the modern languages.

Taken together the two policies have been beneficial to most pupils and they have certainly helped to solve the problems of many of the more gifted children who had not been adequately challenged in their previous schools. There have, of course, been children of high potential whose problems have not been completely solved but at least favourable circumstances have been created so that failures may not be attributable to the school.

It should now be clear to the reader that Millfield and Edgarley offered excellent opportunities for a further study of Gifted Children but as there were many children available some choice had to be made. In both schools because of timetable and other administrative difficulties some children could not be considered and so it was decided to concentrate on the children at Edgarley together from one group which would have just entered Millfield from Edgarley. It was hoped that in each successive year it would be possible to follow up the children from the Junior to the Senior school but this proved difficult and was ultimately abandoned. In the final year of the study all efforts were concentrated on Edgarley partly because it was easier to get a reasonably homogeneous group on the timetable and partly because it was felt that it was more important to deal with the children and their problems as early as possible in their school careers. In consequence of this decision one of the groups of pupils in the final year had an age-range from nine to eleven years.

The problem of choosing the groups had still to be solved. In some cases the school was aware of the IQ of the children as they had been tested by psychologists who had provided a copy of their report. The tests normally employed had been the Terman—Merrill (1960 revision) and the Wechsler Intelligence Scale for Children (the WISC). In other instances the children had sat a group test and the results had been supplied to the school. There were still other children who showed marked ability but who had not apparently been tested. It was decided, therefore, to apply a group test to all the children at Edgarley and the test chosen was the AH4. This test had the advantage of being new to all the children and it had the further advantage of being partly verbal and partly figural. Although the youngest children would not be included in the experimental groups they sat the test because we were thinking of future groups. There were, however, two drawbacks. One was that no norms were available for children of the ages we were testing. The second was that the correlations with the scores we already possessed were less helpful than we had hoped.

When the scoring of the AH4 had been completed it was decided that from the intellectual point of view the children should be chosen firstly from those who had scored highly on the Terman—Merrill or the WISC and on the AH4. Then came those who had done well on a group test and on the AH4.

Thirdly came those who had scored highly on the Terman—Merrill or the WISC but who had not done so well on the AH4. Finally there were those who had done well on the AH4 but for whom no other score existed. Of the thirty-one children chosen six came into the first category, three into the second, ten into the third and four in the fourth. Five children were on our border-line for both intelligence tests and they did well on the tests about to be described. The remaining three children performed modestly on the AH4 but did well on Creativity.

There were three reasons for making use of Creativity tests as well as the intelligence tests. The first of these was that there was evidence, as, for example, in the work of Getzels and Jackson and of Liam Hudson, that children who did not reach the heights in intelligence tests often had other abilities which were not readily measured by intelligence tests, whether individual or group. These tests have a bias towards closed systems of thought and so the youngster who is more capable in open-ended systems is unfairly dealt with. Secondly, experience at Brentwood College of Education had shown that a very interesting group of capable children could be chosen without using orthodox intelligence tests. Thirdly, we were claiming to study Gifted Children and so we must not use too restricted a criterion.

Having made the decision and being aware of the difficulties associated with the testing of Creativity we settled finally on two activities. The first of these was an essay with a so-called "divergent" title, an activity easily arranged for all the children and one which could easily be fitted into an ordinary timetable period so that there would be no need for any undue upset of the timetable or of the children. It was learned later that few of the children chosen for the groups suspected that the essay which they had written long before had any link with their being chosen for membership of the groups. This meant that some of the very bright children were inadequately stimulated as they regarded the essay as just another school exercise to be performed just well enough for acceptance by the teacher in the usual way.

The children were allowed to choose from four titles. These

were: The Monkey That Flies; The Cat That Talks; The Girl Who Plays Football; and The Lion That Could Not Roar.

The first of these titles was easily the most popular and the third was the least and was usually selected by boys. When the essays had been completed they were sent to the author, who had to work out a system of scoring. After recourse to the current literature on the subject he decided to award literal marks under six headings. These were: Fluency (the number of ideas), Originality, Relevance (full use of the title), Fantasy, Humour and Technical Construction. The six marks would then be combined into a composite mark. The scripts were then sent for a second marking to the late Mr D. Moir, Headmaster of a primary school in Suffolk, who was very interested in the problems of Gifted Children. When the two sets of marks were put together it was found that of the twenty-one children chosen for the Edgarley group, eleven received a mark in the B or C categories. Of the ten who scored less than C seven had high IQs.

The second activity was the completion of sets of the Torrance Tests of Creativity. These tests had been developed some years earlier in the United States and were in the form of printed booklets. It was obvious to the children that this was not an ordinary school activity but it was explained to those who sat the tests that the school was trying out some new ideas. There are two types of test: Thinking Creatively with Words and Thinking Creatively with Pictures. Both are rather time-consuming in the scoring and so it was decided to give the tests only to some fifty children who seemed most likely to be chosen for the groups. The tests were on the whole enjoyed by the children, some of whom were to try them again later as part of the regular programme. Thinking Creatively with Pictures proved the easier to score and was always the more popular. It was also the more helpful to us but it must be confessed that the results did not correlate well with the essays and they did not play any great part in our final choices. This is not necessarily an indictment of the tests: they might well have been more helpful if we had had the time which they required for marking and interpretation.

When the groups had been duly formed the author met them

for the first time in the following September, one group of eleven being at Millfield and the other of twenty-one being at Edgarley. After the first day the Edgarley group was divided into two sub-groups largely for administrative reasons. It became obvious immediately that the different arrangements at the two schools were going to affect our plans. In the first place the Millfield group was to meet outside timetable hours following a sports afternoon, whereas the Edgarley meetings were to be timetable commitments. To the Millfield children the experimental meeting was something extra and not to be taken too seriously; to the Edgarley children the meetings were to be treated as seriously as any other timetable commitment and were to be judged for effectiveness in the same way as any other lesson. In Millfield there was less likelihood of the period being regarded as a waste of time; except for one day pupil, the period could be treated as a means of filling in the time between the end of games and the departure of the coaches to the outlying houses. In Edgarley the periods took up time which could have been used for other subjects, with the result that some children felt that they were "losing" time, while others were pleased because they were missing a subject which they did not like: in one or two cases there was tutor-pupil incompatibility, so that the experimental periods provided some relief from real or imaginary tensions.

The second difference was that in the case of Millfield the group was to be taken by one person, a stranger to the children, whereas in Edgarley the teaching was to be shared by the Headmaster and myself, and later another teacher shared in the work. The fact that the Headmaster was involved had obvious advantages in that the children tended to regard the work as schoolwork, if a little out of the ordinary; moreover, from the beginning there was no sense of trying out the newcomer, who was one of the team. There were, of course, disadvantages too, in that much of the material of the course was meant to be confidential and it was hoped that the children would not be too much on the defensive in answering tests and questionnaires which covered attitudes to school and to the routine of school. Further reference will be made to this fact, but generally speaking the disadvantage turned out to be much less than was anticipated, a tribute to the atmosphere generated by the teaching team.

At Millfield, where it had been arranged that I should attach myself for admininstration purposes to the Physics Department, of which the Head was a parent of one of the original Brentwood children, I was introduced briefly and a reference was made to the book, *Gifted Children and the Brentwood Experiment*. This revealed immediately that my interest was in Gifted Children, and I had to explain that these boys and girls had been picked as a result of a series of tests (I did not state at that juncture that they had been chosen very largely on a high or a very high IQ score). At once the question was raised as to whether I was contemplating the writing of another book, and, if so, would they appear in it? The reply was that this might happen but that it was not very likely for a long time to come. One boy asked whether he might read the book about the Brentwood experiment (he was an omnivorous reader) and he duly read and returned it.

The preliminaries over, it was time to make the youngsters do something so that a businesslike atmosphere would be created. Most of the boys and girls had been at games, and now they were prepared to relax. At the same time, one could recognize the existence of mixed feelings. On the one side there was the feeling that this was an extra taken by an outsider and of no great consequence, and on the other side the feeling that this had been sanctioned by the authorities and so it might be advantageous to defer judgement. On the excellent old teaching principle that the youngsters must be made to write something, paper was distributed and they were invited to answer a questionnaire about themselves. This was inevitably, at this stage in the proceedings when a proper relationship had still to be established, largely of a formal nature, but it provided certain information which was vital to the conduct of the experiment.

The first question was the child's full name, but the second was the name by which each boy or girl preferred to be called. One boy remarked that this was an unusual question and he thought that it should be asked by every teacher when he first met his pupils. His remark led to a favourable reaction on the part of the others. Their addresses were sought partly because some of the children had parents overseas and the effect of separation had to be considered. Moreover, some spent each holiday overseas with their parents. The question on country of birth was included for much the same reason: apart from the pride most people have in the land of their origin, there was the fact that in the school itself over forty nationalities were represented. In only three or four cases in the Millfield group had the children been born overseas or still had parents overseas. The next question concerned the number of schools they had already attended, where these schools were situated and for how long each had been attended. Several of the children showed fairly frequent changes of school, and there was the possibility that some of their academic or social problems stemmed from these changes. Information was sought also about the age of beginning to attend school, because many bright children are ready for school by the age of three or so. While this question has usually considerable significance, this was not so helpful as it might have been in more settled conditions. Where there was Nursery School or Class provision, some of the children had attended. Some of the children born overseas had had some provision for schooling before the age of six, others had not. The majority of the children had gone originally to Local Education Authority schools and had been accepted at the normal age of five.

One question concerned the number of siblings and the position of the children in the family. Research has shown that there are advantages and disadvantages in being an only child, or one in a family of three or more children. The only child in a stimulating home has usually much more opportunity for intelligent adult conversation than the child who spends most of his time in the care of or with older children. The child in the large family has often compensation in the social mixing and in learning to get on with and accommodate himself to other children. These ordinary problems occur in families with gifted children but there are sometimes complicating factors which tend to be overlooked and which may yet be of such importance as to affect the lives and careers of the children concerned. For example, two of the pupils at Edgarley showed a good deal of insecurity although

both had IQs of over 150 on the Terman—Merrill. In both cases
there was an older child who was further on in the school course,
in Millfield, and who was doing very well indeed. The younger
children were constantly comparing their own performances,
actual and imaginary, with those of their siblings. In these two
cases, the younger children were as bright as the older ones and
capable of achieving the same standards at least, but it was very
difficult to persuade them that this was so. This growing-up in
the shadow of older brothers and sisters is a commonplace,
especially where the older children are brighter than the younger,
but insufficient attention has been paid in those cases where the
children concerned are all bright. Mr George Robb has referred
to a case where a child with a maximum score on the Terman—
Merrill has been threatened by a younger child who is still
brighter. So far, this has not shown itself in our groups, but
there are pupils in Millfield who do feel threatened by one or
two of the Edgarley children. In another case, the third child
in a family is quite bright, and in the normal household would
have been the star, but unfortunately for him there are two
scintillating stars ahead. The youngster has solved his problem
by opting out of any possible competition in subjects and activities pursued by the older children, and by doing very well in, for
example, practical subjects where there is no hint of intra-family
comparisons.

Other questions concerned the attitudes to the various subjects. In the case of the Millfield children, some were already
taking GCE "O" levels, while others would be taking several a
year later. At this stage there were some marked biases towards
Science or the Arts, but most were taking several subjects so
that the biases were not of immediate significance. More important in some ways was the query as to whether one should write
down a subject as a dislike because the current tutor was not
well liked, or was regarded as one of the less satisfactory ones.
It would have been interesting to follow this up, but one can
hardly ignore professional etiquette. The tutors had their opportunity to record a verdict on the youngsters later on in the
term.

Questions on favourite sports and hobbies produced a variety of answers, revealing that about half were keen on sport while the others put up with certain activities as a necessary evil. Two or three of the boys were tremendously keen on electronics and pursued their studies at home during vacations. Their literary interests were orthodox and in most cases not to be distinguished from those of their coevals. As far as choice of career was concerned, apart from some bias towards Science, there was little evidence that these youngsters had seriously thought about the matter; for the majority, several years of school and college still lay ahead.

To return now to the first meeting of the Millfield group. The session was concluded with the boys and girls being invited to solve a reasoning problem, which some succeeded in doing before the period ended. It was noticeable that some did not start the problem and so it was decided that the second session would be given over to such problems with close observation of the reactions of each youngster. But what was most obvious at the beginning of the second session was the way in which the group had arranged itself. The two girls attending at this stage had paired off (they were already a pair) whilst three of the boys had teamed up and a fourth was loosely linked with this trio. These boys made remarks to one another and tended to be very childish indeed: when three boys of 13+ and of high IQ decide to be childish they appear almost infantile. When the new problems were set, the majority settled down to the work, some with a certain amount of success. These problems were based on the kind used by Valentine in his Higher Reasoning Tests, so that they contained either too much information or else too little. In the former instance, the solver had first to eliminate the irrelevant item, and in the latter he had to be content with an indeterminate solution. These problems proved to be rather difficult and there were signs of exasperation in three or four cases. It became obvious that generally speaking these children had become conditioned to problems with definite and reasonably neat answers. Some produced elaborate and complicated non-solutions and others gave up the struggle. After some help, most managed to find the answers. One boy failed to start for almost fifteen minutes despite some cajoling, and one wondered how a boy of maximum IQ could take so long. Here was a case for further investigation, especially as the part completed, when he had eventually set himself in motion, was perfectly correct. If he had been marked on the quality of the work done, his score would have been 100 per cent; as it was, he had completed only a little over half the work, with a score of 55 per cent. On inquiry from his other teachers, it was learned that this was his customary approach to work, so that in examinations he did well once he had started, but of course he failed to make full use of the time available. Clearly, this was one problem which had to be tackled. Another problem was the alteration of some of the attitudes of some of the pupils, but this will be dealt with in later chapters.

The differences of approach and of the circumstances at Edgarley have already been mentioned. Once again, after a brief introduction by the Headmaster to the two sub-groups together, the two sub-groups divided and the same questions were asked as at Millfield. Twenty children were present, of whom eighteen had been born in the United Kingdom, one in the United States and one in Kenya. Only one was an only child, the majority being from families of two or three children, and two being from families of six children. Ten of the children were first in the family, seven being second, one third, one fourth and one fifth. Of·the ten children with very high IQ scores, seven were the first children in the family. Ten had previously been at only one school, four at two schools, four at three schools, one at five schools and one at six. In all cases they had spent at least two years in one of their schools. Ten had gone to school for the first time at 4+ to 5: eight had gone at 4 and two had had Nursery School experience at the age of 3. Five of the children of highest IQ had begun attending school by 4 years of age.

As at Millfield, the children wished to know whether, in answering the questions on favourite subjects and subjects disliked, they should put down as dislikes those subjects in which they found some incompatibility with the teacher. They were told to ignore this temporary situation. The resulting likes were widespread over the range of the subjects; the dislikes included Latin (there was some doubt about its value) which was well represented also in the list of likes; dislikes also included Mathe-

matics (chiefly by girls) and Music (chiefly by boys). There was
no obvious bias towards either Science or Arts subjects: in
Brentwood there had been a bias towards Science subjects. Most
children claimed to have some hobby, Reading and Stamps being
among the commoner; Archaeology was mentioned once. Most of
the children still liked reading comics, in which there was a fair
amount of exchange. School and detective stories appeared in
the list of favourite books, but one or two preferred books of a
technical nature, linked to their hobbies. Tastes in television
were fairly wide, several children writing "Various"; others specified Comedy or Tomorrow's World. On Radio, Pop or Radio 1
led the list: there was only one reference to the Music Programme
(Radio 3). Five stated that they rarely if ever listened to radio.
Five had no vocational ideas at all, one mentioned Child Care,
two Teaching, three the Services, and two boys mentioned Football but suggested other possibilities as well. The archaeologist
thought of Surgery as an alternative to his first choice.

While there were no signs at Edgarley of the behaviour and
other problems such as had manifested themselves immediately
at Millfield, there were doubts almost from the first about the
expenditure of time on a non-examination theme. These doubts
were to grow despite the involvement of the Headmaster which
in most instances would have been a guarantee of the importance of the course. It was decided, therefore, to take the parents
into our confidence, with the result that the letter described in
Chapter 4 was sent to all parents of the children concerned.
This was useful in its way, but it was insufficient: hindsight has
shown that the children should have had a much fuller explanation of what we were trying to do, even if some of the explanation
had been a little beyond their understanding at the time.

2

Attitudes and Behaviour

When Leslie Smith interviewed one of the small Upminster boys at Brentwood for a radio programme, he asked the boy whether he knew his own IQ. The boy replied that his mother had read the part about the Brentwood Experiment in the book *Gifted Children*, by Branch and Cash, and had told him that the range of IQs in the group was from 130 to 170. Leslie Smith then asked which end of the scale he came nearest, and the boy replied that he believed he had an IQ of about 130. His actual score had been recorded by the psychologist responsible for applying the Terman—Merrill 1960 revision as 170+++. On the whole it was true of the children in the Brentwood Experiment that they did not think of themselves as outstandingly clever or intelligent: in so far as they did indulge in any self-assessment, they tended to think of themselves as quite good at much of their school-work, but they had certain difficulties. On another occasion, a boy, again of IQ 170+, was asked whether he thought that the work which he was set in school was just right for him, or whether it was too easy or too difficult. His reply was that he found the work easy on the whole: he thought that it was right for most of the class but that it was too easy for four other boys and himself. All five of the boys attended Brentwood College; all had scored over 160 on the Terman—Merrill test. Nevertheless, although all found the work pretty easy, none thought of himself as of outstanding ability.

With this experience in mind, it was decided to find out whether similar attitudes prevailed at Millfield and Edgarley. Obviously, it would have been unwise to ask the children straight out whether they considered themselves as very clever, since

modesty, whether genuine or assumed, would have led to guarded
or non-committal statements, and also because at an early stage
of relationships there is not yet the foundation for the confidence required for straightforward answers. In these earlier days,
indirect techniques were used: reactions were sought to certain
stimuli. The setting of some simple logical problems led to a
certain amount of frustration, and in both Millfield and Edgarley
very bright children explained that they were not clever enough
to undertake such reasoning problems. The introduction of one
or two problems in which Maths occurred brought forth, especially
from some of the girls, the affirmation that they were no good
at Maths or Arithmetic. Even when it was pointed out to them
that the Arithmetic processes were extremely elementary, some
of the children were not persuaded that they were capable of
performing the necessary processes. After help had been given
in a number of instances so that the problems were successfully
solved, there was no feeling amongst some of these children that
they were clever enough to cope with the types of problems set.

Further evidence could be adduced from the general attitude
to exams and exam subjects. Although for the majority, probably
for all, there was no need for anxiety since it was clear that the
Common Entrance and GCE should present no difficulties (in a
few of the cases such exams were likely to prove a very inadequate challenge), yet several of the children manifested anxiety.
Some of this arose undoubtedly from the influences of homes
in which they were constantly exhorted to work hard; some
arose from the very common tendency of teachers to remind the
children that unless they worked hard there would be a poor-
quality result. At Edgarley the cause of anxiety, in some cases,
was the fact that the children were setting themselves a target,
namely to try to equal the performance of a member of the
family who had already passed through the school. It showed
itself again when some of their work was criticized as being
unadventurous. When it was pointed out to them that some
examiners regarded an unorthodox approach to a question or
essay-title as an oasis in a desert of mediocre and uninspired
answers, some of the children replied that they were urged by
their teachers to treat exams with caution and not to attempt

anything in the way of boldness. One or two claimed that they had had the temerity to try being adventurous with unhappy results. Some were prepared thenceforth to try a more unusual approach in any suitable work set in the experimental groups but none seemed to be convinced that it was, after all, a feasible technique in any of the ordinary subjects or examinations.

Later in the second term the children at Edgarley were given a brief questionnaire asking whether they regarded themselves as very clever, clever, or just above average. Nobody claimed to be very clever; just over half thought they were clever; two failed to answer and the remainder settled for just above average. As this was written and could be regarded as confidential (the children had been assured on several occasions that anything they communicated would be treated as confidential and not transmitted to any of their teachers) there seems to be no reason why the answers should not be accepted as representing their actual views.

In a society in which there is a tendency for people concerned with education to assume that too much is already done for bright children, who are capable of making their own way and who are already especially favoured, it may be hard to realize that in reality many bright children do lack confidence in themselves and in their abilities. This lack of confidence is very considerable in some cases and shows itself in a variety of ways over a wide range. The commonplace belief, especially of girls, that they are incapable of success in Maths has already been referred to, as has the tendency to become anxious about exams. Lack of confidence showed itself in an inability to talk in front of other members of the group, even where taciturnity was by no means observable in other class-room situations. The possession of a wide vocabulary and abundant knowledge on a theme were insufficient to compensate for the firmly entrenched lack of self-confidence. It manifested itself at times in the brevity of the written work (more will be said of this presently under the heading of "the stint"). This occurred on several occasions, especially with the boys, who had plenty of self-confidence as long as they were dealing with maths and other factual material, but who found it difficult to produce even the very low mini-

mum set in imaginative or literary work. The origins of this lack
of confidence varied, some deriving at least partly from the
home, and some from the school situation itself. The children
manifestly lacked a basic understanding of themselves and of
their capabilities: a lack which pointed to needs which will be
further discussed in Chapter 9.

At Brentwood, one of the most conspicuous characteristics of
some of the bright children had been their keen sense of humour:
quite often so effervescent and ebullient as to constitute a menace
to law and order if it had been allowed full play in a large, ordinary class. Much of this humour was quite mature and it was
often linked with a keen appreciation of the absurd or incon-
gruous. There was less evidence of this humour in both the
Millfield and Edgarley groups, but it did and does exist. In both
the divergent-title essays and in the Torrance tests there had
been flashes of humour, but on the whole it was less spontaneous
than with the younger children. Perhaps as one approaches the
period of exams in life, one becomes more serious or feels that
fun is out of place in school; perhaps the work was not adequately planned to release the springs of humour, but the fun only
occasionally emerged. On the other hand, many of these youngsters were much less restrained outside the class-room. When
certain well-attested humorous stories were read to the group, the
children seemed to accept much of this as humorous, but they
did not react as they might have done outside: in other words,
it tended to be approached as just another school activity.
Nevertheless, the younger children saw this particular activity as
being different from the normal timetable activities and they
ultimately designated the "lesson" as "QK" — otherwise, "Queer
Kids."

Some reference has already been made to the attitudes to
subjects: the attitudes on the whole were favourable. Certain
subjects were accepted as essential for careers and for life
generally, the outstanding subject in this respect being English.
It was perhaps significant that this subject appeared on no child's
list as being too difficult or too easy, when the Edgarley group
was invited to state which subjects they liked best and in which
they found the work either too easy or too difficult. In three

or four cases Latin was stated to be, on occasions, too difficult:
one or two thought that it was too easy and not very challenging,
Maths appeared most frequently on the "too difficult" list,
but the stress was on "occasionally" rather than on "often."
Divinity was appreciated by a few, mainly girls, who were planning to take the subject in their GCE, but it was the subject
which received the largest number of dislikes. Evidence of this
hostile feeling showed itself at other times: for example, when
the children were asked to complete Richardson's Study of
Values, some of them, even in the process of filling in their
answers, said rather impatiently, "This has far too many questions on Religion." Their actual scores on Religion will be dealt
with later when the test as a whole is discussed. But, these likes
and varying degrees of difficulty apart, the children tended to
accept the curriculum without much criticism or evaluation.
These subjects were the normal ones studied in schools, they
were the subjects on which they would subsequently be examined
for the GCE, they were those from which a final selection would
be made for "A" levels and possibly for University or College
later. When the time arrived to offload some of the subjects, the
earlier dislikes would play their part. So would utility, and for
the majority Music would be abandoned at the first opportunity.
In some cases also, the determining factor would be teacher-
pupil incompatibility, but the teacher-pupil relationship was
obviously always relatively temporary so that a year later views
of a subject might well be different.

In both Millfield and Edgarley the attitudes towards the
school were generally favourable: as for most boys and girls of
10 to 14 years, school was a natural part of their lives and so
it was accepted without much serious criticism. Amongst the
boarders there were some who would have preferred to be day-
pupils and perhaps two or three children did not regard school
too seriously. Some of the children realized that they had a
responsibility to their parents who were paying for their
schooling, whilst others, who knew that they had been granted
a remission of at least part of the fees, appreciated that Millfield
and Edgarley had helped their parents and themselves towards
a solution of their educational problems. Those youngsters

who had not been very successful in their previous schools, where, largely because of numbers, they had been denied the help and challenge they required, seemed grateful for the opportunity they had been given. They were not completely uncritical, but with one or two exceptions they believed they were better off in their present school than they were likely to be in another school. For example, one girl who had had experience of three or four small primary schools found Edgarley and Millfield a kind of haven where she could settle down to live and work with other children of her own ability. One of the boys who was most emphatic in his preference for Edgarley over his previous schools had, despite an IQ of 170 and an early entry to school, been kept in the top section of the Infant department because it was felt that he was too small and too young to accompany his older class-mates to the Junior school when he was rising seven. In Edgarley, at 9+, he was working with 11-year-olds. It is, perhaps, significant too that some boys and one or two girls stated that they found school-life more interesting than life at home during the holidays: there was, at least, always something to do at school.

This relatively uncritical acceptance of school by children who could be devastatingly critical in other ways (in some instances, for example, of their parents and, in others, of adults generally) applied to some extent also to their acceptance of teachers. As indicated above, there were inevitably certain incompatibilities which became the subject of commentary, even where the children were warned that for professional reasons they must not mention names, even to a non-member of the staff. All seemed to be aware that teachers, like children, varied considerably in ability. In Millfield, where there was a good deal of latitude in the choice of teachers by pupils, the author has overheard discussions on which tutors one should try to join in the various subjects. Comments such as "He often makes mistakes on the blackboard," or "He is very woolly!" or "He takes half the time to get himself organized," were not uncommon. Such shrewdness is not peculiar to boarding-schools but in such schools the children meet teachers playing different roles in the school and the boarding-house. The bright child could, perhaps, sum up a teacher more quickly than some of the less bright would do, but the real difference almost certainly lay in the greater demands that the bright children made, often without being aware of the fact. Their knowledge and capacities were greater and their expectations higher than those of children of lesser ability, so that there was more chance of a teacher being weighed in the balance and found wanting. Despite this, however, the teachers were accepted as such and the children reacted largely in the way that most children do. On the other hand, only one in five of the children thought that they would like to become teachers, and when they were asked to write down the names of a few people now alive whom they admired, teachers occurred but rarely in any of the lists.

Attitudes to the work in school, apart from the dislikes already mentioned, seemed to be favourable. Opposition to a subject came usually from some inability to master parts of it, or from failure to get on with the teacher. Only one or two raised the question of whether a subject such as Divinity was worthwhile in the curriculum. This general acceptance of the work was comprehensible but seemed to require further analysis. For this purpose it was decided that the reactions of the children to the concept of "the stint" should be tested. It had already been noticed that these children, like those at Brentwood, if given a minimum number of words for a composition, wrote a paragraph or so and then counted the words. Most of them achieved the minimum, say of 250 words. with signposts along the way, such as 50, 90, 150, etc., words. The approach was the same as at Brentwood, to ignore the topic as such and produce a stated number of words. This behaviour led to the idea of reading a passage from *Gifted Children and the Brentwood Experiment* and seeking the reactions of the children: the most appropriate passage seemed to be the following, on the idea of "the stint":

> The most obvious of these was what we in Brentwood have come to call "the stint." Most of our children quickly showed that they had become accustomed to responding to a certain expectation, and they were so used to it that they thought

our expectations would be the same. When we asked the children to write, they would ask how many pages, or occasionally lines, we expected, and they were expert at providing the quantity suggested. The quality was treated in much the same way, and some of the children were quite taken aback when we showed dissatisfaction with what they were accustomed to hand in. For example, on one occasion one group was asked to write in 100 words, as interestingly as they could, about themselves. Fairly typical of the responses was the effort which follows, written by a boy of IQ 170:

> I am a boy of almost ten years. I usually wear my school blazer, short, grey corduroy trousers, grey socks and black shoes. I attend . . . Primary School and have reached Class 3. My teacher is a man who may be about 35 years of age. I like the school mostly, but I also like to go home at night when I sometimes watch television and sometimes go to the swimming bath. After another eighteen months I shall be leaving this school and going to a secondary school, but I do not yet know which school it is likely to be.

The young author certainly produced his hundred words, but one feels the effort of it in the details about his clothes and the spinning out of the last sentence. He was eminently satisfied with his work when he handed it in and seemed quite surprised when he was informed that it was rather disappointing, and that, although it conformed to the quantitative condition, it was far from being interesting. In other words, it satisfied the idea of the stint, and there was no call for anything different or better.

Two questions were posed as guides to the ensuing discussion. These were:

(a) Does the idea of the stint apply to your work in school?
(b) Would you advise the Headmaster to admit the boy who wrote that composition?

On the first question, most of the forty or so children who were submitted to this exercise agreed that the stint played a part in their work, but several different reasons were adduced. For example, some maintained that it depended on the boy or girl — such children were content with a piece of work which would pass muster with the tutor or teacher concerned. Others said that in every class the children of average ability set the standard of the class, with the result that the work of the brighter children did not require to be of very high quality to be accepted as satisfactory. A third view put forward was that it depended on the subject or activity: where the child was interested, the stint would not operate, but wherever the work was too easy or there was boredom, the stint would be very noticeable. A fourth suggestion was that the stint usually depended on the teacher: if he set a high standard, the bright child would respond; if he was content with a mediocre standard, the stint would undoubtedly come into operation.

Here are some samples of the view in the children's own words:

A boy states: "I think that this [the stint] is quite true 90 per cent of the time."

Another boy answers: "Yes, in a normal class you are expected to do average work like the rest of the class. But when you are expected to do better work but still on the same standard of work, you keep on at the same standard as a normal class, doing work which, by your own standard, is bad, but for a normal class or person of your age is good."

A third boy: "I think that what is in the book is partly true. This happens in some of our essays. People usually do this [the stint] when they don't know much about the subject, or it is boring."

A girl gives another viewpoint: "I think that it depends on the person. In myself I think that there is a 'stint' in some things that I do. Mostly, I am afraid of what is going to happen if I don't do enough, but if I know that the tutor will not get mad with me, I don't mind at all."

A second girl says: "Partly true, but depending on which subject. In some subjects, I know what is expected of me and I do not do any more than I know the tutor expects."

On the whole there was little sign of any appreciation of intrinsic interest or motivation, leading children to do considerably more than expected. Except in games, or other so-called extracurricular activities, the tendency was to do what was asked, sometimes well and sometimes merely adequately. Several of the children had hobbies which they pursued with great enthusiasm: there "the stint" did not apply. There, other thoughts occasionally showed up, but the children found them hard to express clearly. For example, one boy remarked "Yes, to a certain extent 'the stint' applies, but it is sometimes otherwise, and it is especially otherwise on the Rugger field!" This is a clear enough statement, but the following one requires a considerable use of the imagination to understand what the boy is trying to say: "Sometimes the stint applies. If you do an amount of work which is good I think that you should try to make your work as good as you can, unless you have to do a certain amount." This boy seems at least to be seeking the distinction between quantity and quality.

In the answers to the second question, (*b*), there was quite a cleavage of opinion. An older group was almost unanimous in declaring that the boy who wrote the essay should not be admitted to Edgarley on the evidence provided, since, apart from the high IQ, the description he gave of himself conveyed little information. It is interesting to note that few of the group realized that they were equally liable to write in this correct but rather boring way and that they might not have been admitted themselves, if admission had depended on an essay of similar type.

A younger group took a somewhat different approach. Most agreed that the essay as it appeared was neither informative nor attractive. One girl expressed doubt: "I do not know. All he has told us is that he wears such and such, watches telly, goes to the swimming-bath and likes his school. I don't know." The majority came down firmly on the side of admission, not be-

cause of the qualities the boy had shown, but because Edgarley was a great place for a boy with such a high IQ score. For example: "Yes, I think he should be admitted, because with an IQ of 170 he should (if he came to Edgarley) be able to use it more efficiently. It sounds in the passage as if he doesn't really try, but could do much better." And a girl thinks: "Yes, he should be admitted to this school because I think it would help him to develop his good subjects to their highest measure."

From the adult point of view perhaps the most interesting feature is once again the failure to relate their own views about themselves and their school to their views about the admission of another child. The majority, who, as had already been shown, were happy in their school of which they thought highly, regarded it as a place which would stimulate the unimaginative essayist and make him work up to the standards suggested by his high IQ. This was expressed in the same period and almost immediately after the same children had largely subscribed to the opinion that at least in some parts of their daily studies they were themselves not being adequately challenged or obliged to work up to the standards suggested by their own IQs. It is doubtful whether any of the children, at this juncture, were aware of their IQ ratings, as these, where they were available, were not communicated to them, but they were aware that they were members of the special experimental groups because they had performed well at some time or another on certain tests. Thus, while they often underestimated their powers and capabilities, they were aware that in much of their school work they were more successful than most of their peers or coevals. In consequence of this exercise it became clear that these children still required a good deal of help in the process of coming to understand themselves and in clarifying their ideas.

In the Brentwood experiment, one of the weaknesses was the difficulty of maintaining an adequate liaison with the schools from which the children came, with the result that we lacked information about these children in the class-room situation. Details were supplied by Head teachers in some cases, and sometimes by class teachers, but in other cases the supply of information was meagre. Obviously, in a boarding-school the

problem of obtaining information was greatly diminished, but there were certain difficulties. One of these was that staff were busy with reports and other paper work just at the time that the information which we were seeking became necessary to the experiment. Another was that, because of the tutorial system, it was found necessary to seek information from over fifty tutors about the eleven children then in the Millfield group. These circumstances offered one advantage and at least one disadvantage. The advantage was that reports would be obtainable from a considerable number of tutors in full, while for each pupil there would be several reports, so that any cases of incompatibility would probably be evened out. The disadvantage lay in the form that the reports would have to take. In order to reduce the time required for this task to the minimum, the report forms would have to be streamlined, and the categories would have to be fairly broad and very carefully chosen indeed. As it turned out, there was a splendid response from the staff, some of whom supplied additional information which proved most helpful.

When the form was devised, it was geared to the answering of five questions which seemed to be significant for the understanding of these children, keeping in mind that in a group of high ability there was no need for any of the children to play down their ability for social reasons. The questions ultimately decided on concerned:

(a) How the children appeared to the tutor in his subject: were they very bright, bright, average, or below average?
(b) The children's performance in their subjects: very good, good, average, below average.
(c) What were the attitudes of the children to the subjects: favourable, indifferent, unfavourable?
(d) What was the standard of behaviour of the children in their respective groups: very good, good, average, under average?
(e) Whether there was any evidence of under-achievement.

Because of the essential brevity of the pro-forma, no definitions of any of the terms was attempted (all the tutors were requested to do was to underline one of the choices in each

question) but despite this the results, especially in Millfield, proved very interesting indeed. The number of questionnaires returned was 104, the highest number for a pupil being 12 and the lowest 7. Of the 104 tutors, 32 said that the children appeared "very bright," 51 said "bright," 19 said "average" and 2 said below average." One tutor remarked of a certain pupil that he had never thought of him as Gifted until he had received this questionnaire, while another said of a boy (IQ 160+) that there were other cleverer children in his group. In only one case (another boy of IQ 160+) did all tutors responding agree that he was very bright; in two other cases (boys of IQ 154 WISC and 166+ Terman—Merrill) the tutors underlined "very bright" or "bright." In all but one of the other cases (a boy of IQ 160+ who had one "average" but also one "below average") there were at least two tutors who thought of the children as of average ability.

In considering the answers to question (*b*), it is well to keep in mind that all of these youngsters were likely to take some "O" level papers well before the age of sixteen, and so the tutors' judgements were based on a good "O" level standard. The figures are again very interesting. Of the 104 reports, 20 said that the performance was "very good," 43 that it was "good," 6 that it varied between "good" and "average," 23 said "average" and 12 said "below average." One must remember also that very few children who are taking a wide range of subjects are equally good at or interested in all, but for a group of high potential, such as this was, there seemed to be too few "very good" replies. Only three pupils had no "below average" answers, and only one no "average." One girl (IQ 170) and one boy (IQ 160+) had three "very good" performances. The boy with the lowest IQ score (140+ Terman—Merrill) had two "very good," one "good," five "average," and one "below average" returns, which must be judged more than satisfactory for nine reports. One boy, the slow starter mentioned earlier, had one "very good," five "good," one "good to average," and one "below average": there is little doubt that if some means could have been found to galvanize him into starting test papers and essays more quickly, his report would have been very different; one tutor remarked "What he does, he does well, but he never does enough."

The third question, about the pupils' attitude to the subject, did not produce much of interest. Of the 104 responses, 87 were for a favourable attitude, 15 for an indifferent attitude and two for an unfavourable one. It is possible that tutors might hesitate to state that their pupils were unfavourable to their subject, but on the whole the pupils revealed in other ways that indifference was more common than an unfavourable attitude, since they would soon opt out of a subject they disliked.

Expectations of teachers as to the behaviour of children in their classes vary considerably, but in answer to question (*d*) most of the tutors were satisfied with the behaviour of the children in this study. Thirty-six reported the behaviour as "very good," 32 as "good," 29 as "average" and only 4 as "under average." The groups were small in comparison with those normally found in Local Education Authority schools, in which some of the bright children inevitably have less attention than those at Millfield. The four pupils who figured in the "under average" column were all boys. Only one pupil, a boy, had all his reports in the "very good" or "good" columns.

In the fifth question the tutors were asked to say whether there was some evidence, or else no evidence, of under-achievement. Out of the 104 replies, 61 suggested that there was some evidence. This tied up largely with the way in which the children appeared to the tutors (question (*a*)) and with their estimates of performance (question (*b*)). The lowest returns under "some evidence" were 3 out of 9 replies for a girl, and 3 out of 7 replies for a boy. Two boys had 5 (out of 9 and 12 respectively), 4 children had 6 (out of 9, 10, 9 and 8), one boy had 7 out of 11 replies, and the record-holder had 9 out of 10 replies. This last result described, once again, the boy remarkable for his slowness in starting, and thus was complementary to his reports on question (*a*) (5 "very bright," and 5 "bright") and those on question (*b*) (1 "very good," 5 "good"), out of 10.

A briefer analysis should suffice for the results of the same questionnaire when applied at Edgarley. One must keep in mind the fact that the Preparatory school was very much smaller than the Main school, and so there was in some ways a closer link between the teachers and pupils than in the much larger senior school. This greater intimacy would have certain advantages in that the teachers saw more of the pupils and so could apply more pressure to secure achievement according to the teachers' estimates of potentiality. Against that was the possibility of a somewhat more subjective approach and in some cases at least, a more defensive approach: not self-defensive but rather one of protecting the pupils against possible outside criticism.

In question (*a*), the number of "very bright" reports was 49, that for "bright" was 92, for "average" the number was 13 and for "below average," 1. Considering the range of ability and IQ scores, these results were a little surprising. One girl (IQ 147 WISC) who tended to underrate her abilities, did not appear very bright to any of her teachers: she seemed to be "bright" to 5 and "average" to 2 of them. A boy (IQ 154) did not appear as very bright, but he was acknowledged as bright by 7 of his tutors. Unlike the girl, this boy had some appreciation of his cleverness and was somewhat aggressive, tending to call out in class, sometimes with rather cynical remarks. All the other children without any reference under "very bright" were at the lower end of the IQ scale.

In question (*b*) most performances were described as "very good" (34 in all) or "good" (95). There were 22 "average" performances and 5 "below average." One boy (IQ 152) had 3 "good" and 5 "average." The girl previously mentioned (IQ 147 WISC) had 3 "good," 3 "average" and 1 "below average," while the boy also referred to in the previous paragraph had 5 "good," 1 "average" and 2 "below average." These apart, the children lacking a "very good" performance were again at the lower end of the IQ scale.

In question (*c*) the attitudes were overwhelmingly favourable. Only 5 "unfavourable" and 3 "indifferent" were recorded. In question (*d*) the majority were said to behave very well (88); good behaviour was reported in 49 cases; average behaviour, which was obviously regarded as unusual, was reported in 16 cases, while "under average" occurred only three times. The boy of IQ 152 referred to above had one average and two under average entries: he was undoubtedly somewhat unconventional. The aggressive boy had one average and one under average return.

In question (*e*) there was a great majority in favour of the statement that there was no evidence of under-achievement, a verdict which did not entirely agree with the views of the children themselves. There were only 35 reports of signs of under-achievement. It is, perhaps, significant that only 2 children had a zero in the under-achievement column; 9 had only 1 for under-achievement, 5 had 2, 2 had 3 and 2 had 5. The unconventional boy was one of those with 5, and the girl who under-valued herself also had 5. There was still enough evidence to justify looking further into the problem of under-achievement.

3

Programmes

One of the first problems to arise was that of whether a programme should be devised as the basis of the experiment, but
it was decided to dispense with a regular programme for a number
of reasons. Firstly, there was the limitation of time, only a mere
two periods each week being available for the groups. Secondly,
there was the degree of specialization in subjects: there seemed
to be no point in choosing work directly connected with any
subject which was already being taught on a specialist basis and
within which, because of the tutorial system, the children were
already at different stages. There were also good professional
reasons for not poaching on anyone else's preserves. Thirdly,
there was the very limited staffing of the groups, most of the
teaching and testing having to be undertaken by one person.
This limitation in staffing also made it difficult to explore the
borderlines between various subjects, such as had been attempted
between Arts and Maths, for instance, in the Brentwood experiment. Another argument against devising a regular programme
was the existence of another experiment, that of Professor
Tempest, for whose group of Gifted Children, in Southport,
programmes had been devised, which were to be published at
the end of the experiment. These would almost certainly help
teachers of gifted children in the class-room situation in a way
in which a much more limited study would not do.

The conclusion was that the experiment must remain exploratory with a variety of activities which would be determined
partly by needs already known to exist and partly by needs
which would disclose themselves in the course of the experiment.
This approach would allow a great deal of flexibility, but ob-

viously, with the small amount of time available, the investigation in any one field would be very restricted. The first step, therefore, was to survey the information already acquired about the children and to settle on what seemed to be the primary needs of the groups.

Even before the children were chosen for the original groups, it had become evident that there was some evidence of under-achievement, evidence to become much stronger later, as has been made clear in the previous chapter. We knew from earlier experience that the term "under-achievement" covers a number of conditions arising from a variety of causes. In our studies we were concerned chiefly with a fairly narrow section of the spectrum of under-achievement. Most of our children had shown the ability that is measured by reputable Intelligence Tests, and we felt that we were entitled to expect evidence of this ability to a high degree in their scholastic performances. Most of them were performing satisfactorily as long as they were regarded as clever or bright children, but we were prepared to argue that performing satisfactorily was not tantamount to performing according to their proven ability. We were not looking for all-round brilliance since research[1] has shown that while the majority of children who score very highly on an Intelligence Test are reasonably good all-rounders, they are rarely equally brilliant over a wide field of subjects or activities. We suspected that the good performances of at least some of the children were the enemies of very good or excellent performances. Our suspicions were to be justified in several cases and in several subjects, and so we came to the conclusion that more intellectual stimulation was required: this must be regarded as one of the basic needs.

Immediately the question arose as to how this basic need of intellectual stimulus could be provided within the framework of the school and its normal objectives. One suggestion was that the children should undertake a wider range of "O" levels than pupils of lesser ability. This was already tending to happen, so

[1] G. Peaker, *Incidence of Polymathic Giftedness*, quoted in Schools Council Report by Dr E. Ogilvie, *Gifted Children in Primary Schools*: Schools Council Research Series, published by Macmillan.

that it was likely that the children in the groups would later acquire strings of "O" levels. At first sight this seemed to be a natural solution to the problem, but when one remembered that we were seeking greater intellectual stimulation, the solution did not after all seem to guarantee that increase. For highly intellectual children, "O" levels cannot be regarded as of sufficiently high level to satisfy their needs. Their thinking is, and has been, at adult level. Thus, unless one is prepared to go outside or well beyond the usual range of "O" level syllabuses, there is a danger that one may aggravate rather than solve the problems of these children. On the assumption that all children who hope to enter a profession, or some occupation of equivalent intellectual status, require a sufficiency of passes in the GCE at "O" level, these children should certainly study a number of subjects and sit the appropriate examinations, but six or seven subjects at that relatively low level should be adequate for any very bright child.

Possibly, time might be made available for other activities likely to match the children's adult capabilities. In any such intellectual activities they would be in groups with their peers, whereas in their "O" level studies they would in many cases be likely to be with children whose pace of work and quickness of understanding might be very different from theirs, consequently impeding opportunities for intellectual stimulation.

Another suggested solution to the problem was that the very brightest children should by-pass "O" levels and proceed to a higher standard as soon as they had given evidence that they were ready for a further advance. This would inevitably mean that they tackled a smaller number of subjects but that the work would be much more intensive. This seems an improvement on the first suggestion, provided that one keeps in mind the entrance qualifications to higher education and to professions, which in our present social set-up do require consideration. One must also guard against excessive specialization, which is often dictated at a still higher level because of the fantastic growth of knowledge, as for instance in Science. Somewhere in our society there must be some compromise between depth and breadth of knowledge. Curricula tend by their nature to be restrictive and

exclusive, and these effects must be guarded against where they
may become harmful to the student, who must ultimately be
helped to live a fuller and more abundant life. Perhaps the inevitable compromise will be of another kind: that certain parts of
the curriculum will lead to necessary examinations while others
do not. To make such a compromise workable, whether for gifted
children or for the less gifted, it would be essential to reorientate
much of our educational thinking and both parents and teachers
would require to work together to create a fresh approach to
school on the part of the pupils — a mammoth task.

Another possible solution would be to undertake some work
with the very bright children outside the regular school programme. This has several advantages and possibilities. Firstly, it
means that the children can be brought together for part of the
school week on a basis other than subjects in which they are
preparing for specific examinations. This basis is that all the
members of the group will be gifted in one way or another.
Most of the children will have performed highly in some tests
and in the group it should be possible for the results of the
tests to be given and their meaning or value explained to the
children. For example, several will have performed very successfully on an Intelligence Test: they sometimes know the actual
score, which they may tend to interpret. They should be shown
that this score points to the possession of certain abilities and
these abilities can be made the basis of their lives in the future.
At the same time it should be made abundantly clear that the
tests have their limitations, and that there are external factors
which may affect the result favourably or otherwise if the test
is repeated under different circumstances. There is usually an
opportunity at this point to refer to certain simple statistical
techniques, such as means and standard deviations, which make
it possible to compare the results of tests and exams. Insight of
this kind into the nature of their abilities seems essential for all
youngsters: it is urgently necessary for those who are outstanding
in any way above their coevals, since, as we have already seen,
the children in quite a number of cases are troubled by their
outstanding ability.

For the majority of the children there is a marked development in the power of abstract thinking and conceptualization. They may follow roughly the Piagetian steps of development but they certainly reach quite a high standard of abstraction at a much earlier age than the Piaget experiments suggest. Indeed, in some cases, there are signs of impatience with teachers who adhere too strictly to concrete approaches. An example of this from a child of six (IQ c. 150) at Brentwood illustrates the point. The boy was already able to think abstractly in terms of numbers and he showed great resentment when a student-teacher insisted on his using Cuisenaire rods, which he had clearly outgrown, to work out calculations which he had already worked correctly in his head. Some of the children in the experimental group showed a similar impatience with an outside speaker accustomed to talk to people who required a certain amount of repetition of ideas, with examples; the children remained polite but one could see that several were tempted to say, "Yes, we understand. Please pass on more quickly to your next point." If a teacher can make them aware of the reasons for their feelings of frustration in such circumstances, then they will understand themselves and their powers better and in consequence may become more tolerant of those whose powers are less or else lie in a different field. The lesson, of course, must be carried still further, to the tutors normally responsible for teaching the children in their subject groups, so that as far as possible the work may be made more challenging. Meanwhile, one of the functions of the groups in special activities must be to continue the intellectual stimulation of the children and the setting or provision of tasks and studies that will make fuller use of their gifts.

Another advantage of groups for special activities is that both directly and indirectly one can tackle the problem of reversing the conditioning which has been affecting the gifted children from their early days at home and school. Apart from the few whose parents have an exaggerated view of the capabilities of their offspring, often at an absurdly early age, gifted children, as we have suggested, tend to reach a plateau in their intellectual development, and often parents and teachers fail to encourage them to climb still further towards the summit of their powers.

The children soon discover that they can perform the allotted
tasks quite well, and as long as their parents and their teachers
are satisfied with their answers and their written work they
continue to perform in the way expected. They can achieve an
exalted position in the class if they feel so inclined and the
reports emanating from the school satisfy their parents. The
larger the class, the more likely that the teacher will be content
with work which is as good as that of any other child in the
class. As indicated in the previous chapter, the teachers may
regard such children as "bright" but do not realize that they
are "very bright." The children themselves have come to believe
that school is an amalgam of pretty easy work and boredom.
Obviously, the longer this conditioning process has been allowed
to continue the more deep-rooted it will be in the children, and
the harder it will prove to eradicate. Some youngsters proceeding
from a Primary school, in which they have performed satisfactorily with little effort, to a selective Secondary school in which
they find themselves in classes with equally bright children, discover that they need to make a greater effort than they have
been accustomed to. This often proves to be a painful process:
in some cases the children have coasted so long that they find
the necessary effort beyond their developed powers or their
peculiar character traits and so they sometimes face failure in
the Secondary school. Fortunately, some of these children make
much greater efforts outside school and their quality of reading
or of scientific studies may be much higher than in school, with
the result that they soon adjust themselves to higher school
standards.

This leads on directly to the further advantage of groups for
special activities that one is able to tackle the problem of the
low level of aspiration of many gifted children. In the case of
those children who are far more energetic, inventive and creative
outside school, there may well be two quite different levels of
aspiration, and whenever the higher level is outside the school
then the school becomes a less important factor in their development. Such a case is that of a young girl, as related by George
Robb, who asked her mother, on her return from school, why
she had to stop thinking each day during school hours. Schools

must either offer a fresh, challenging approach or else cease to encumber such children, who will realize much of their potentiality otherwise than through school.

It is more serious for those children who tend to accept the level of aspiration from outside, from parents and from the school, as the norm, and assume other children are, like themselves, content with a modest performance. The day arrives when they accept what is good enough for others as good enough for themselves. They are often aware that there is something wrong but they are not always able to analyse the position in which they find themselves. Others reach the stage where effort does not seem worthwhile and the long-term result may well be some more highly intelligent drop-outs. In the small peer group, with regular exposure to intelligent adults who have applied their talents with enthusiasm to their professions, vocations or hobbies, there is an opportunity to make these youngsters realize that their efforts are inadequate and that there is the possibility of an absorbing interest in at least some of their work and activities. If this inward vitality can be awakened or reawakened, then it is possible to replace the old, relatively low level of aspiration with a new, higher one. Something must still be done to make certain that the environment is sufficiently stimulating to ensure a progressive development of the inner forces of the children: in other words, the new effort must be twofold and must come from a new, challenging school atmosphere as well as from within the children themselves.

Another clamant need of many of the very bright children is for help in growing up in a balanced way so that the emotional and social development match the intellectual development. Of course, this is a general need of children, since they all have to achieve a balance if they are to live a worthwhile life. There is no suggestion here of any forced growth, although there are trends in our present-day society to turn boys and girls into little men and little women, contrary to the teachings of Rousseau. Moreover, many children, whatever their intellectual ability, grow up to become well-balanced adults: indeed, some of them are amazingly mature even as children. The author has come across a number of cases of very bright children, especially girls, who by the age of 10 or 11 were emotionally and socially quite adult. But this does not apply to all, so that many children of high intellectual development are relatively less developed emotionally and socially. In such cases the imbalance of development aggravates the problems of growing up which are common concomitants of the gradual progress from childhood to adulthood. Sometimes this imbalance reveals itself in what adults tend to call pertness or an undesirable perversity. At other times it betrays itself in extreme sensitiveness to criticism, or in a tendency to isolation, or in regression which seems out of place and extremely childish to any person accustomed to judge the child according to his intellectual ability.

Bringing together very bright children for even a small part of the school week has several advantages and functions. Firstly, those with emotional and social problems can meet others of much the same intellectual ability who have largely solved the problems of a balanced development. This can and does have a stabilizing effect on such youngsters since they have satisfactory examples before them from whose experience and behaviour they can themselves learn. The contact may well teach valuable lessons where the children with problems contrast their own reactions to provocative situations with those of children of more balanced development.

Secondly, the contact with others whose problems and state of development are similar can make it possible for children to begin to appreciate that they are not unique but that others have to face the same difficulties as themselves. In this way they can be helped to realize that their own problems are relatively commonplace, and several may join together to consider these difficulties and to assist each other, both to understand the nature of the problems and to seek solutions.

Thirdly, partly as a result of these contacts, and partly as a result of the help which can be given by an adult, whose function is to succour the youngsters, these children can make considerable progress towards self-understanding, which is the basic requisite for a truly adequate and balanced development. It is unlikely that this contact will be fully successful unless it is accompanied by contact with other less intellectually gifted children and this contact must embrace both working and playing together. In other words, the very bright children must not regard themselves as different: they are children whose problems may take a somewhat different course from those of other children. In being helped to a more accurate assessment of their abilities and strengths, the very bright children must also be assisted to an understanding of their weaknesses.

This help will call for a programme which will embrace philosophical ideas, including one's personal aims. This does not necessarily involve a formal study of philosophy as such, but it is surely necessary that the children should be helped to become aware of how they make decisions and why they tend to behave in certain ways in a variety of circumstances. They require to see and to evaluate their personal behaviour as a reaction to occurrences outside themselves over which they may have little or no control and also to the behaviour of other people, for example parents, teachers and other children, whether in the family or in the school or in any other organization. They require to be led to understand the meaning of values and value judgements, and also to be helped to discover, on occasions, the sources of these values which they have adopted, in most instances without thinking or being conscious of the process. Some appreciation of the emotions and of how they affect values, behaviour and reactions whether to beautiful or provocative stimuli, would seem essential. Much of this appreciation should obviously arise in the course of the ordinary school studies, such as Literature, Divinity, History, Languages and so on. The material can be supplemented from a study of hobbies and other outside interests and probable future professional interests may be harnessed as an incentive.

Another great need for some of the children in the experimental groups was help in establishing satisfactory relationships with other people, often including their schoolmates. Two facts should, however, be kept in mind. Firstly, some of the children were well developed socially and so were able to establish and maintain good relationships with both children and adults. Secondly, several of the children had been sent to Edgarley or

Millfield because of the difficulties they had experienced in their previous schools where their outstanding ability had posed problems both for their teachers and for themselves. Some of the aspects of the problems discussed below together with the illustrative cases underline several failures to find solutions in earlier years. In several of these cases no blame can be attached to the previous schools as they were not equipped to cater for such children, and furthermore there has been a tendency nationally in education to ignore such problems or at least to fail to analyse them adequately.

Some of the children showed signs of insecurity which intensified their need for the company and friendship of other children and the greatness of their need sometimes led to desperate attempts to acquire friendships. This type of case may be illustrated from the experience of a Headmaster who is at present trying to solve a problem facing a 5+-year-old girl in his school. This girl entered his school at the age of 5 years, but with a reading age of 11 years. She had picked up reading largely by her own efforts. The Headmaster, who has been interested in the problems of gifted children for a number of years, at once obtained readers suitable to the ability of his pupil, and he arranged that she should come to him each day for reading and for discussion arising out of the reading. So far so good, but now, when the girl is with her own age-group, she refuses to read the books at her own level and insists on sharing the very simple readers that her class-mates are using. Her desire and need to be like them is too strong for her to accept the full challenge of her own powers. The Headmaster in consequence finds that he still has to solve his problem.

Though none of the cases in the experimental groups posed such a severe problem as that of the little girl, the same need did exist. For instance, one boy of considerable ability but with an intense feeling of insecurity was constantly seeking to establish relationships with some of the older children. Unfortunately, in his desperation and in his inexperience in dealing with other children, he chose as the object of his friendship two other boys who had their own social problems. To the outsider it was apparent that he could not have made a more injudicious choice as the three children were fundamentally incompatible. Inevitably the boy's approaches were repulsed, sometimes in a manner which caused him a great deal of distress. There were other children available who would probably have reciprocated his approaches, but he failed to see this. The best that could be achieved by us at the time was to try to point out to this boy that he would at best have to be content with a state of neutrality between himself and the other boys, and that he should seek his friendships in future with other children.

Most of the children have passed beyond the infantile stage when the bright child is often domineering, insisting, for instance, that games, which he may have devised, must be played according to the rules he has instituted, otherwise they will not be played at all. One or two showed signs of a continuance of this tendency to domineer but by now it had become a tendency to patronize others of alleged or apparent lesser ability. This showed up very little in the experimental groups themselves since these were specially constituted, but it did manifest itself in the ordinary school groups and in the activities outside the classroom. In one experimental group one boy showed signs of childish arrogance at the very beginning of the experiment, but his lack of success in a task of a logical nature soon reduced him to a realization that there were others in the group who were superior in certain respects to himself. Later on, but not necessarily *post hoc ergo propter hoc*, he became quite successful in the task which had led to his greater humility.

Another social problem showed itself in two or three cases where the children deliberately isolated themselves from other children. The most noticeable case in this category was that of a boy who was very much happier in reading than in any activity requiring co-operation with the other children. There is, of course, a need for all of us to isolate ourselves at times, to give us an opportunity to meditate and to think creatively, so that some measure of isolation is both justified and necessary. This need undoubtedly applied to this boy, but his devotion to books and to being by himself was excessive. There were clear indications of a deep personality upset, which originated outside school, but which was not, unhappily, being given the attention it required.

In these circumstances his intellectual abilities were being very markedly restricted and would be so until he could overcome his personal problems.

The commoner forms of isolation were those in which the children found it difficult to establish satisfactory relationships with their coevals, or were rejected, as shown in the sociometric choice, by their coevals. These cases can be sub-divided into two categories, those who were genuine isolates and those who were only apparently isolated. The latter were isolated in their groups but were able to establish relationships with other children or with adults. Such cases were not very serious, since the children found companionship outside the classroom: at home, in the case of the day pupils, and in other activities in the case of the boarders. Even so, there may be problems since the age disparity may be such that it is not possible to make rearrangements within a school for these children to work together. Some of the children suffer a blow when the older children with whom they have established contacts leave the department for a higher one or for another school. Vertical grouping may help in some of the cases where there is a modest age disparity, but in a school run on a subject basis the studies pursued by the children can be so different as to make any group adjustments difficult. For those who seem to require adult contact, there is much to be said for clubs or activities which will involve such youngsters and understanding intellectual adults working or studying together. The bringing-in of such adults to school can be helpful. An example of this was shown by two boys who always found it almost distressing to express their opinions in front of their classmates (they were practically isolates, on a sociometric test in their class) and yet, when outside speakers came in to talk to the groups, they showed none of their usual inhibitions but asked questions freely and responded readily to questions asked by the speakers. They seemed hardly to notice the presence of the other children, some of whom, for a while, found themselves deprived of their customary leadership.

The second category of isolates covers a variety of forms of isolation which can best be illustrated by reference to certain actual examples. For instance, there were those children whose

interests were quite different from those of the majority: some
children had no interest in the games, even when they were
allowed a free choice from a long list of possible activities; they
either eschewed games because they lacked any of the fundamental skills required for success or enjoyment, or regarded
games as childish and in consequence a waste of time for them.
Although there is evidence from Terman and other sources that
very bright children are often of all-round ability, excelling in
games as well as in academic work, some very bright children
find themselves, like many other children, to be of moderate or
of slight skill. Such children were well represented in the experimental groups. Whereas several of the children looked forward
to their sports activities or followed the fortunes of some notable
Soccer Club or Rugby team, others had no interest at all. One
very bright boy with a near maximum IQ, whose own relatives
were keen on a famous football club, could not understand
their addiction, so that he was as isolated at home as he was at
school. A lack of interest in sports, or an active dislike, did not
seem to bring the children together: they tended to increase the
isolation of those who were not fortunate enough to find some
other common interest.

Although many of the children were very fluent, one cause
of isolation was the disease of compulsive talking; a disease more
dangerous, probably, where so many children responded readily
to any stimulus. One such pupil, who had clearly been brought
up to express views on a vast variety of subjects, was on the
whole unpopular because, whatever the circumstances, she had
always something to say: her delivery was invariably confident
and her remarks trenchant, whether the statement on which she
was commenting had emanated from an adult or from another
pupil. Despite her domineering tendency, she was not without a
sense of humour and could take a joke against herself. The fact
that much of what she did say was quite sensible almost certainly aggravated the feelings of hostility towards her and in fact
accounted for her low score on a sociometric test in her experimental group.

Finally, there were those who were regarded as somewhat
abnormal, even in groups of children who designated themselves

as "Queer Kids." There was, for example, the boy who tended to interrupt a serious discussion in a childish way: he was told off several times by other members of his group and once or twice, when he was absent, the other children passed on the news of his absence with marked pleasure. After two terms or so, he seemed to perceive that his behaviour made him unpopular and he gradually quietened down. Another boy, whose adolescent ambivalence was extreme, so that he might behave like a small boy one day and like a mature adult the next, might be described as a part-time isolate. A sociometric recording taken on one of his odder days showed him as an isolate; another, taken later, in a more mature spell, showed him with three chums, including two mutual choices.

In marked contrast, there seemed to be little isolation resulting from intellectual rivalry or feelings of envy: those with the highest and those with the lowest IQ scores seemed to be reasonably popular in the groups and outside.

4

Other Problem Areas

On the whole an outsider would have said that the majority of
the children came from what we usually call "good" homes,
offering them affection and stability, whether they were boarders
or day-pupils. There were, of course, instances where the home
was broken for one reason or another and the behaviour and
performance of two or three of the children had undoubtedly
been adversely affected by unfortunate home occurrences.
There were, too, children whose parents were living or serving
overseas, but generally every effort was made to bring the family
together at suitable times, such as the vacations. The number of
children whose work and behaviour were seriously affected
seemed to be very small indeed. It is improbable that the proportion of children affected by these conditions was any greater in
the experimental groups than in the school population at large.

There were, however, some "good" homes where both parents
were alive and present, which, if not causing some of the difficulties of the bright children, were certainly aggravating them:
this was apparent from the fairly common view held by these
children that parents and teachers, and indeed adults generally,
were constitutionally unwilling to or incapable of listening to
what their teenaged children were saying. Most of the children
thought well of their parents apart from this general parental
weakness. Nevertheless, some were critical in a perceptive way.
For example, one boy, an only child, came from a doting family
which included the grandparents as well as the parents. This boy,
on one occasion, on being asked if he were looking forward to
going home for the vacation, answered that he was except for
one thing. In response to the query as to what his reservation

was, he said in a sarcastic tone, "As soon as I arrive home, I lose several years and half expect to see my mother getting my pram ready." There was evidence that at home he was still regarded as a very small boy and that the parents were unwilling to see him grow up. Some of his difficulties in establishing a suitable rapport with children, and even with teachers, understandably arose from this source, aggravated by the fact that he was also the intellectual superior of his parents.

Another boy, again the only child, came from a home where the parents had very high expectations and were obviously hoping that their gifted son would go considerably farther in the world than they had done, although they were both intelligent people. They had realized quite early in their son's life that he had a high potential, and after taking advice they had concluded that he would be better off at Edgarley than in the local Primary school. The boy had acquired, somehow or other, a conviction that the work done in an ordinary state school was largely a waste of time, and that he should always be studying at a high level. But there had been some kind of revolt, with the result that he seemed often to be suffering from lassitude. Although his school work was for the most part satisfactory, in most subjects it was below his potential. One or two of his teachers expressed some doubts about the trustworthiness of his IQ score, but the test had been carried out by a most competent psychologist. One teacher said of him that he had started off well in class but had dropped marks rather badly in the end-of-term tests. He suggested that he was under some stress on his transition to the larger senior school and that he required more practice in examination techniques. He was sometimes slow in picking up certain aspects of his particular subject. Another tutor asserted that it was easy to underrate the boy; there was evidence that he was capable of better work than he sometimes produced. There was sufficient proof, from the various tests that he sat in the experimental groups, that he was a boy of considerable ability who had lost most of the urge to work up to his capability, and there can be little doubt that the source of his difficulties was the home.

While some parents had faith in the schools and contented

themselves with supporting them in a variety of ways, or with encouraging their children to make full use of the opportunities offered, there were occasional instances of parents of very bright children being dissatisfied with the schools and usually also with the performances of their offspring. Such parents tended to overlook the fact that their children had perhaps been accepted because certain problems were not being solved or given adequate attention in schools with a less favourable teacher-pupil ratio. For example, one pupil who had some personality difficulties which manifested themselves in reading problems, was sent on the advice of an educational psychologist. His performance was patchy at first, but he began to make much better progress: all ten teachers reporting on him agreed that he appeared "very bright" or "bright." Despite this marked improvement, the parents were still dissatisfied with their son's progress and they felt, no doubt in all sincerity, that the rate of progress might be accelerated and that certain long-standing weaknesses might be remedied by taking certain specific steps. Perhaps there was justification for their analysis, but it overlooked two important factors. The first of these was that the boy had certain social problems, which would not be solved merely by increasing the intellectual pressure. In any case, the house system was already playing some part in his development. The second factor was his reaction to his parents and their attitudes. Their attitudes were not confined to the school, although their animadversions on the school were disturbing to their son, who, as is so common in adolescence, had developed a high degree of idealism which contrasted with their much more practical and experienced views. A reconciliation of the views of parents and son seemed unlikely but it was obvious that the boy probably would not overcome his handicaps and develop his potential until both parents and child came to a greater understanding of each other's attitudes. He was far from convinced that their action was for his good: they were really sure that they were really trying to help him.

As stated above, most of the children seemed to find their parents encouraging and helpful, apart from those differences which are now styled popularly but very inaccurately "the generation gap." There were, however, in some cases, anxieties about parents which led on occasions to a feeling of worry or malaise. Whether it was because of absence from home or for some other reason, some children (not all boarders, incidentally) expressed the wish that their parents might have an easier time. The father was mentioned rather more frequently than the mother, as if the children had been reading some of the newspaper advertisements for life insurance. In one or two instances where the mother was mentioned, the anxiety arose from the fact that the ladies in question ran a family and also undertook outside duties which kept them busy. In discussion it was possible to point out or hint at the fact that where one has a housewife of high intelligence and great vigour it is beneficial for health to undertake a variety of interesting activities which make much more use of abilities than does a household which is already running smoothly.

Other problems arising from the home derived mainly from sibling relationships. Reference has already been made, in Chapter 2, to the difficulties of younger children following highly gifted children through a school. In the school itself, teachers often unconsciously assume that younger children from a family of bright children will perform as well in a subject as their older brothers and sisters. This is an unfortunate assumption, since the younger children may have different gifts from their siblings or else may be hindered by the dominance of the older children. At home the older children who have already made their mark tend to be the favoured ones and some of the children in the experimental groups were resentful of this. One boy went so far as to declare that he preferred school to his home because he was tired of being treated as an infant by two older teenaged brothers. His school-work was obviously not affected by his brothers, but his boldness in class seemed to be some sort of reaction to his none too willing submission at home. A girl, whose older brother was doing very well indeed in his scholastic work and on the sports field, tended to feel inferior in the school setting, and showed some anxiety in consequence, which understandably affected her performance. This feeling of inferiority seemed to have been exacerbated by the attitude of the parents and of the older boy, who all appeared to subscribe to the view that boys were superior to girls, so that, while some appreciation of her reasonably good school-work was shown, most of the praise and admiration seemed to be directed towards her brother. Whether this was in fact so or no, this girl accepted it as true and suffered accordingly.

There were one or two cases of children who, as the eldest in the family, with a good intelligence, had found themselves entrusted with responsibility for younger siblings at an age when most of their coevals were free from such responsibilities. It is not suggested that young people should not be charged with such tasks, since to be put in a position of trust helps children, and especially very bright children, in the process of growing up to be adults. But where too much responsibility is given a child, because he seems to be the possessor of an old head on young shoulders, there may be some harm done. Two of the children, at least, seemed to have become ultra-serious, partly as a result of this experience: here again there was evidence of mixed feelings about the holidays.

In the course of some of the discussions it became clear that the children were still rather puzzled as to the purpose of the weekly periods even although most of them had by that time accepted the so-called Queer Kid periods. While some of the doubts manifestly arose from the children themselves and especially from those who were most concerned with their examination prospects, others arose from the attempts of the youngsters to explain to their parents what they were doing. Some of the parents seemed to expect a kind of inventory of what had been done in all subjects throughout the term: others obviously paid much less attention and assumed that the school authorities were responsible beings who would not allow a wasteful usage of term-time. In an effort to help those children who were experiencing some difficulty at home it was decided that a letter outlining the function of the periods should be sent out by the Headmaster to the parents of all the children of the Edgarley groups. In this letter several points were made.

Firstly the parents were told that their children had been included, for one or two lessons each week, in one of two special groups which contained some children who were gifted in some way. There was, however, nothing in the letter to indicate whether their particular boy or girl was regarded as gifted. Secondly it was stated that the work undertaken by these groups was somewhat different from what the children normally did during their other lessons. The third point was that some part of the programme was concerned with helping the children to reach a deeper understanding of themselves as persons. At the same time an attempt was being made to assist them to a greater understanding of their relationships with other children and with adults. Finally the parents were asked to treat this approach to their children seriously and to encourage their offspring to develop a favourable attitude to the programme since it was directed towards helping their children to grow up into balanced adults.

It was hoped that a number of purposes would be served by the letter. It provided a rationale for the expenditure of a certain amount of time in trying to satisfy these parents, who were doubtful about any activity that did not seem to lead to specific examinations. It was felt also that if the parents treated the experiment seriously then in most cases there would be a better response from the children, and so the activities would be rendered more valuable generally and more useful to them as individuals. As the letter emanated from the Headmaster, who was participating in the activities, the experiment became official. Indirectly, we hoped, there might be some sort of helpful response from the parents which would assist us in helping their children. We did not, however, invite a response which would in any way seem to impose an obligation on the parents to write back to us about their children. In the event, a small number of parents did write in the most encouraging manner and none responded adversely. Some mentioned the letter to their children and seemed to accept the experiment as a normal part of the school-work. A few parents took the opportunity offered by Open Day to raise the matter: in at least one case the parents considered that this additional study of their child should increase the value of any advice given to them by the school. One proposed that regular reports should be submitted on their children, but it was pointed out that there were certain difficulties. The parents already received regular reports covering performance in academic work and in extra-curricular activities, on behaviour in the classroom and in the houses, for boarders, so that there was in each instance a number of tutorial opinions and assessments. Would there have been any real value in a report that would have been tentative in nature and sometimes merely echoing what other teachers had already said? Another objection to reporting on children in the experimental groups was that they had been promised that whenever they were expressing genuine views or revealing their own thoughts the material would be treated as confidential. To have included some of the material in reports might well have led to further tensions in the school or home since it would usually be all too easy to trace the source of the information. Clearly, in some senses, a dilemma occurs: unless the children are convinced that their views will be treated as confidential they will be on the defensive and so will not reveal what may be troubling or handicapping them; on the other hand, if their revelations cannot be communicated to anyone, then the chance of providing them with help in overcoming some of their difficulties, or in solving their problems of relationships, is greatly diminished. Perhaps this is one of the strongest arguments for having in each school a counsellor who is independent of the normal school hierarchy.

Some children, whether they had problems at home or no, did find certain problems in the school, but it is unlikely that the numbers were abnormal in any way. The attitudes to the school were in the great majority of cases favourable. There were children who found it difficult to keep to all the rules and a few who thought the rules silly and unnecessary, but there was no evidence of strong feelings in this matter. There were, of course, some teachers who were generally regarded as more efficient and effective than others, especially in the art of preparing pupils to pass examinations, but this kind of judgement is to be found in any school, amongst children more or less gifted. There were incompatibilities of teachers and children because of different behaviour patterns and expectations, but there was nothing unusual in this. Two or three of the children were rather eccentric and likely to be sources of disturbance even in small groups but this can occur in any school population. In one such instance, a tutor reporting on a boy remarked that he was often a nuisance but likeable withal. References to tutors by name were strongly discouraged on professional grounds but on the whole the teachers referred to by the children were almost always those whom they regarded highly. There were, of course, the cases, already mentioned in Chapter 2, where children had ceased to like a subject because it was now being taught by a tutor who was not liked, but these were more than balanced by cases where children, after stating their dislike of a subject one year, declared the same subject, taken by a different teacher, to be their favourite the following year. One very bright boy said he did not think much of his teacher in a certain subject because he sometimes misspelled words on the blackboard. It was most interesting, therefore, to discover that when that teacher reported on the boy he said he was very bright, and performed excellently, except for his eccentric and original spelling.

Although there were ample opportunities for the boarders to express views on their school houses, there was little response on the whole. Occasional comments were made, and these were more often favourable than otherwise: again there was evidence of acceptance of the conditions as normal in boarding-school, and usually in accordance with what one reads in school stories. The few difficulties that there were arose more from the children than from the house-masters and mistresses, despite considerable differences in expectation. There were the occasional expressions of resentment, but these were directed towards the senior pupils rather than towards the adults. As usual some boys and girls in office tended to make too full use of their authority according to the younger children, but there was no evidence that this tendency affected the lives of work of children in the experimental groups in any serious way. There were inevitably children who were incompatible in the same house, and in at least one instance this did affect the happiness and the school-life of the children concerned, two very bright children who seemed, for a period, to spend a good deal of their time making full use of their talents to upset each other, with apparent success; but since other habits of these two boys were quite well known some limitation of their activities was possible.

When the relative reticence of children about their lives in the houses came up by chance in a conversation, the consensus of opinion of a small group of the brightest children seemed to be that after initial homesickness, and some minor humiliations at the hands of some of the older pupils, life became bearable and on the whole uneventful; that there was not very much worth discussing, and that in any case it was not done to go about criticizing either the houses or the people in charge. They might make remarks or jokes amongst themselves but they would certainly not do so outside the houses.

Now that we have looked at the background of the children in the experimental groups and have become acquainted with some of their problems, it is time to turn to the work which was actually done by and with them. However, it is first necessary to stress certain limitations, some of which have already been referred to. There was no possibility or point in choosing regular work in any of the ordinary subjects, because these were already being taught on largely specialist lines. In any case, the weekly allocation of time was so exiguous that little impact could have been made through any subject. As indicated earlier, some of the children found some of their subjects rather uninteresting, and more of the same subject might well have made them less co-operative. A further good reason for eschewing such a course was that it might well have rendered members of the staff less co-operative. These considerations, however, need not be permanent in a larger-scale study in which members of staff work as an experimental team. Indeed, some such development is likely to prove necessary if the brightest children are to be substantially helped.

It has already been suggested that the programme, in so far as it could be so designated, was to cover three main fields, intellectual activity, self-awareness and awareness of others. Intellectual activity covers all work requiring a high degree of intelligence, but it also covers those activities which tend nowadays to be included under the heading of "Creativity." Not much has been said so far about Creativity and its investigation, but the reader is reminded that Creativity tests played a part in the selection of the first groups. A separate chapter will be given to those activities which were intended to stimulate or explore Creativity. At this point, however, it is important for the reader to bear in mind that most of the activities could be dealt with under more than one heading. As far as possible they will be described under the heading appropriate in each case to the major purpose. All the activities were intended to have two functions: firstly, they were supposed to be of such a nature and of such a quality that they would stimulate the children to work at a level nearer their potential than they were accustomed to do. Secondly, they were supposed to be exploratory, so that we should find out more about the children, their responses, their attitudes, their interests and the drawbacks to their realizing their apparent potentiality.

In dealing with the various activities I shall begin with those related to the intelligence, since most of the bright children were chosen largely on their high IQ, and, since it illustrates the point made at the end of the preceding paragraph, the first reference will be to the Concept Mastery Test. One of the first problems facing us was to find a reading test which would give us a realistic assessment of the reading ages of the children. At Edgarley we tried out the Watts Reading Test but it proved much too simple even for our not so bright children. Other reading tests met with not much greater success. As the test had to be a real challenge and also exploratory, we turned to the Concept Mastery Test. There seems to be a chronic shortage of tests suitable for bright teenagers and one tends to be obliged to use adult tests devised for Senior High Schools in the USA. Unfortunately, while these tests often provide the necessary challenge, they rarely provide norms for much younger children so that their value is lessened.

The Concept Mastery Test consists of two sections. The first comprises 115 pairs of words of increasing difficulty and the student is asked to indicate whether the pairs are synonymous or antonymous. Obviously it would be possible to guess the answers, but there is a corrective in the scoring, since for each wrong answer one mark is deducted from the total of right answers, each of which receives one mark. The second section consists of 75 analogies in which the student has to choose the correct answer out of three choices, As the element of guessing is reduced, the scoring is one for each correct answer and $-\frac{1}{2}$ for each wrong answer. The children were told of the method of scoring before they began to answer, and this information determined their individual strategies, which varied greatly, as will be shown later.

There are serious drawbacks to the Concept Mastery Test as a test for children about to enter their teens, or in their teens. Firstly, it is very difficult — the pairs of words towards the end are often quite strange to the children and the analogies require a great deal of information which is not usually found to be amongst 11- to 14-year-olds, A second handicap is its American basis — this rankled so with one boy that he wrote the word "Yanks!" on his paper. Thirdly, the system of scoring is gener- ally too severe and depressing for school-children. In some cases it led to excessive caution even when the children almost cer- tainly knew the correct answers. In other cases they knew part of the answer but hesitated to risk the loss of a mark by insert- ing it. This effect was less noticeable in the second section where the penalty for an error was only half a mark. Nevertheless, as will be shown later, the system of scoring had at least one advantage in that it showed a difference of approach from one child to the next, which led to a greater insight into each child's attitude. Because of this difference it was decided to study the number of correct answers in relation to the number of items attempted and percentages were worked out which are shown in the table below. This was a useful corrective in some instances, as, for example, in that of one of the youngest pupils. His total score of $36\frac{1}{2}$ was one of the lowest in the group of 21 children, largely because he attempted relatively few items. In Section 1 he answered only 14, but was correct in 12 of them, and in Section 2 he answered 25 with 24 correct. Without any correction for his age his σ score was just under -1, but his percentage for Sections 1 and 2 were 87 and 96 per cent respectively. These successes were, of course, mainly in the easier items. The lowest score of all was that of a pupil who had more wrong answers than right in the first section, as a result of some optimistic guessing and disregard of the scoring system. This pupil did much better in the Analogies, with 38 correct answers out of 48 attempts. The percentage scores of correct answers were 43 and 79 per cent respectively, a fairer reflection of this child's ability.

Child	Part I		% R	Part II		% R1	Total Score	σ	% R + R1
	Right	Wrong	No. Attempted	Right	Wrong	No. Attempted			No. Attempted
1	22	3	88	27	7	79	$42\frac{1}{2}$	−0.19	83
2	28	3	90	40	5	89	$52\frac{1}{2}$	+0.57	89
3	37	19	66	29	11	72	$41\frac{1}{2}$	−0.27	68
4	34	16	68	30	10	75	$43\frac{1}{2}$	−0.11	71
5	17	4	81	34	25	57	$34\frac{1}{2}$	−0.81	64
6	14	2	87	25	2	92	36	−0.69	90
7	28	10	73	37	6	86	52	+0.53	80
8	40	18	69	29	8	78	47	+0.15	73
9	26	9	74	31	14	69	41	−0.31	71
10	50	16	75	40	14	74	67	+1.7	75
11	67	39	63	44	19	70	$52\frac{1}{2}$	+0.57	66
12	33	2	94	36	5	88	$64\frac{1}{2}$	+1.5	91
13	28	10	73	37	17	68	$46\frac{1}{2}$	+0.11	70
14	28	11	72	27	11	71	$39\frac{1}{2}$	−0.42	71
15	77	32	70	44	13	77	$82\frac{1}{2}$	+2.0	73
16	18	24	42	38	10	79	27	−1.4	62
17	43	11	80	35	36	48	49	+0.31	62
18	29	4	87	27	12	70	36	−0.69	78
19	37	19	63	24	9	73	$37\frac{1}{2}$	−0.57	68
20	35	7	83	20	6	77	45	0	81
21	14	2	87	29	0−	100	41	−0.57	95

When we examine the table we can make certain observations. The first is that there are some very good scores, if we accept 60+ as a reasonable return for the younger group and 85 for the older group. This would give three good scores and two excellent scores in the younger group and four very good and one excellent score in the older group. It is interesting to notice also that some of these scores were achieved by the cautious and others by the more adventurous. On the whole it is obvious that while those children with a really high IQ had some advantage, the correlation with IQ was quite low. Probably the high average IQ of the older group accounted in part for its considerably higher average, 67 as against 48 for the younger group. As already mentioned, age is an important factor in this test when used with children below sixth-form level, but this discrepancy in the averages is greater than would be expected from an analysis of age difference in the younger group.

Actually, in the senior group the mean for the children over 14 was 62 compared with 66 for those under 13, but this is largely accounted for by the pupil who scored 33 and who was in certain ways a special case, not responding to any challenge at the time. The average age of the older group was 13.7 and that of the younger group 12.4. When we examine the results obtained by the younger group in relation to their ages we find that the average score for the under-12-year-olds was 52, that of the 12-year-olds 43 and that of the 13-year-olds 53. The under-twelves all had high IQs, otherwise they would not have been included in the experiment at that time; the two youngest, nevertheless, had quite low scores. In the 12-year-old group two of those with high IQs produced disappointing scores. However we look at the figures, there seems to be evidence that this Concept Mastery Test, with proper precautions, has a use in assessment, but that in at least one respect the IQ individual tests seem to cover much the same ground. The second point for observation is the very marked differences in approaches to the test. Some of the effects of the system of scoring have already been mentioned: quite a number of the children became ultra-cautious. This, however, is not the complete explanation of the differences. Some of the children had quite clearly thought out for themselves the correct tactics, as far as they were concerned, for approaching an examination. Some realized at once that while they would not score highly in an absolute sense, they would be likely to score more highly if they restricted themselves rigidly to answering those questions where they could be certain of correct replies than if they were less selective. There was to be no question of taking what they considered an unjustifiable risk in a relatively unfamiliar context. Normally when sitting examinations the majority of those children would be well prepared and most of the questions would have a familiar look. Where a choice was allowed, they would choose the questions which offered the prospect of quick and certain marks. In a sense, then, they were in this instance merely adapting their normal procedure, but on this occasion it was under the stress of a different form of penalty, should they err. There are the examination candidates who tend to plunge in, taking certain chances in closed-system exams, and often feeling happiest when faced with open-ended questions. There were several such children who in the Concept Mastery Test plunged in, despite the penalties, and tried to do as many items as possible. Honours seem to have been about even, with five of the highest scores resulting from the employment of the first method and the other five from the second method. It is possible that a little less caution on the one hand or a little more on the other might have made an appreciable difference to some of the scores. Of the nine lowest scores, only two seem to be the result of the cautious approach, so that perhaps it can be regarded as the more valuable for those who find themselves on the defensive in such circumstances. It is the people on the defensive, together with the slow-but-sure, who benefit when performance is calculated according to the formula — amount correctly done in relation to the amount actually attempted.

Finally, it is necessary to raise the matter of the use of this test and of the children's reactions to it. The two sections had to be sat on different days, as the periods were not long enough to permit of the whole test being sat at once. This was by no means a disadvantage, as 190 items pose rather a formidable task for children on an adult test. Stimulation varied considerably, from the acceptance of the challenge to "the stint" attitude: that this was another piece of work to be done, without much relevance to the examinations which lay in the future. The challenge was most clearly accepted by those children who attempted as many items as they could in the time allowed: they plunged in and showed on the whole some pleasure in performing the test. Some of those who answered very guardedly revealed a genuine response to the challenge, but others were too preoccupied with their defence to betray any pleasure or enthusiasm. Several of the moderate scorers passed with excessive speed from one item to another; if they had been a little more patient they would have given themselves a chance to worry at some items and so find more correct answers. Such children were only too ready to conclude that the test was too difficult and so they avoided the main challenge.

5

Introductory Activities

The apparent avoidance of a challenge had been noted in the early days of the experimental work at Brentwood College of Education amongst high IQ children. There were some youngsters who were described as "rather lazy" by the teachers in their schools, but on analysis this laziness turned out to be quite different from idleness or indolence. The lazy children, most of them boys, were usually performing well in their ordinary work in class, but they were not prepared to make a greater effort because they seemed to regard what they were doing as adequate. There was no doubt that these children were under-achieving and that they required greater stimulation or fresh incentives or aims. In the College situation, in competition with other children just as bright or even brighter than themselves, they began to respond at a higher level than in school. This occurred fairly quickly in Maths and Science but took considerably longer in language. The demand for a greater "stint" was usually met so that the measure of under-achievement was reduced, even if there was little evidence that the school "stint" was increased correspondingly. In such cases the setting of higher standards of work with an adequate challenge is probably what is most necessary and on the whole the prognosis is good if the new situation can be created in the normal school setting. It is reasonably certain that a good secondary school, which can bring intellectual peers together for at least part of the school week, helps many such children to improve their achievement.

The alleged laziness of some bright children also covers another category in which the problems are more intense and where a much greater effort may be required on the part of teachers. This category includes those who have, partly as a result of chronic under-achievement and partly as a result of prolonged conditioning, developed certain attitudes to work, especially work based on closed systems. If children have been conditioned to believe that all school-work is easy, calling for little effort, and that all problems have one definite answer or solution, then they will approach all work with the expectation of performing it quickly and easily. Several of the children at Brentwood showed this syndrome and when the normal cure of harder work was applied it led on some occasions to resentment and even to unhappiness or despair. These cases seemed to indicate that any teacher taking over children with this unfortunate background of experience would have to devise a course which would help them to accept harder work with the minimum of frustration.

Although in the setting of Millfield and Edgarley, with small groups instead of large classes such as the Brentwood children had come from, it is much easier to study individual children and to determine the stimulus and challenge required, several of the brightest children showed signs of requiring the specialized form of treatment devised at Brentwood. There seem to be at least four requirements. The first of these is the obvious one of more challenging problems than they have been accustomed to confront. Curiously enough, such children will often solve fairly difficult problems if they are set on the Quiz or Problems page of a children's or even an adult's magazine. A number of such problems, of which examples will be given below, are to be found in the very useful book, *Learning to Think*, by E. R. Emmet (for the busy or puzzled teacher there is an excellent "Companion")[1]. The second need is for problems which are difficult to solve, or even impossible to solve definitely because insufficient evidence is supplied. After all, this is a commoner situation in life than the one in which problems work out easily and conveniently have only one possible answer. Corresponding to these but at the other end of the scale are problems in which too much information is available and no solution is possible until the irrelevant information has been eliminated. Such material is to be found in the late Professor Valentine's

[1] Published by Longmans, 1965.

Higher Reasoning Tests: here again one is obliged to make use of material originally devised for sixth-formers and adults. This need, to learn to eliminate the irrelevant, is manifestly basic for anyone who wishes to go on to the higher levels of education and of research: the need to learn to look out for such irrelevancies is just as important and valuable a lesson for any promising pupil. The author recollects one occasion, when he set part of the Valentine Higher Reasoning Test to a group of adult teacher-trainees, when a quite gifted Maths student filled some four or five pages with formulae and calculations in an attempt to solve a problem without eliminating an unnecessary piece of information: if she had noticed the irrelevancy she could have solved the problem in two or three lines. The fourth need is for a considerable amount of open-ended work, but that will be dealt with in Chapter 8 under the heading of "Creativity."

The first problems set (from Emmet) concerned football and cricket, as it was felt that these would at least interest the boys and would not prove very difficult for the girls. Several incomplete league tables had to be completed and the scores of the actual matches worked out. An understanding of the way in which league tables are constructed was assumed, but this assumption was not always justified, especially with younger children or children from overseas. Even the boys who were rabid followers of some of the outstanding Soccer teams did not seem to have discovered, in all their study of the championship tables, that where several teams played each other the total of the goals scored by teams must be equal to the total goals conceded by the same teams. Others did not immediately realize that an entry in the Draws column must lead to a second entry in the same column. Naturally, once they were forced into realizing such facts they quickly mastered the completion of more complicated tables: it would probably have been just as effective to point these facts out, as was done in answering questions in one or two cases. It was shown clearly once mor that even the very bright children do not always perceive what an adult accepts as commonplace: such children still require the teacher to teach them directly or else to place them in a situation where they can learn for themselves.

For most of the children the second part of the exercise, working out the scores of the actual matches, proved more intractable than the first, as few of them had any plan for discovering the individual results. The majority tried some form of trial and error and several of these eventually reached the correct solution, after several tries. In all the groups in which these problems have been set, some children, usually boys, have thought about them before putting pen to paper and have deduced certain principles. One of these is to start with the draws, since they are the easiest to spot; the children using this tactic were amongst the first to come up with a correct solution. Some of these children, and others also, used a tabular form of approach so that they were able to reason in a systematic way; this approach had the added advantage that it was easy to check up on what had been done. In each group, one or two children solved the problems much more quickly than the others but without using any of the commoner techniques. They could not recollect having attempted this kind of problem previously. In at least two cases boys had reached the correct answers very speedily but when they were asked to explain how they had done so they were unable to give what could be described as a satisfactory account. The author has come across this type of thinking in several gifted children. It is tempting to refer to it as intuitive thinking but in this sense that comfortable phrase merely covers our ignorance about a certain process. Teachers sometimes demand an explanation of how such children reach their answers, and if the explanation is not satisfactory they suspect them of copying or guessing. It would appear that some of these children do have ways of thinking which are more complex than those of less gifted people and it is almost a form of cruelty to ask them to explain. If children finish their problems first, then there is no question of copying, and if they solve their problems consist-ently in their peculiar, abbreviated form of thinking, there can be no question of their succeeding by inspired guessing.

The children's reactions to the problems told as much about them as the methods they used. There were several who protested that they were not interested in games and so saw no attraction in making up league tables. They had to be reassured that despite the reference to games the problems were really of an intellectual nature and so suitable for work in school. There were those who were quite unfamiliar with the use of league tables and had to have the basic principles explained to them, thus drawing attention to the nature of the solutions as well as of the problems. There were those, on the other hand, who were interested and felt that they knew all that could possibly be known about league tables, but were somewhat shattered to discover that there were certain features of league tables which had never occurred to them. However, they really enjoyed the exercise and some inquired whether they might undertake some more complicated problems involving a greater number of teams. It had to be explained to them that the addition of even two or three more teams would render the working out of results much too difficult for anyone to be able to do. Some of the more timorous or reluctant ones, on being successful with the first problem, tackled the others with growing enthusiasm and of course with more rapid success. There were, however, some who succeeded only after a certain amount of help from the teacher or from one of the other children, but who were not won over to this kind of problem: so much so, in fact, that when they were informed on later occasions that there would be some number work at the following session, they would exclaim, "No more football leagues, sir, please!"

Through these problems, some of the children had already begun to show a difference of attitude to the work being set: indeed, some wished to continue on the same lines. It was desirable to continue the process of influencing attitudes by ensuring a progression, but a progression determined as much by response as by intellectual development. A simple intellectual progression would have been easier to devise, but some of the children would have lost interest and this would have included several of those most in need of stimulation. The next step must, therefore, not be too difficult but it must have a content somewhat different from the earlier exercises. For this reason it was decided to take examples of another kind of problem, which would allow one to say truthfully that the reasoning was not so very different from what the youngsters had already shown they could do with success.

The first of these problems consisted of statements made by five schoolboys who had been competitors for a prize. Four out of the five statements were guaranteed to be true; one was apparently

irrelevant. The children had to discover what the actual order of
the prize list was. In appearance the problem did not seem to be
very daunting and the children settled down to it quite happily in
the various groups. Some of them reached a solution quickly but
not all checked it before asking whether it was correct. About
half of the children were finished, correctly, within a few minutes,
and eventually all were successful. It was noticeable that some
of the pupils, despite a great desire to be first out with the correct
list, checked the solution against the facts and knew for themselves that they were right. Others, in their anxiety to be first, did
not check, and some were wrong. The most valuable lesson emerging from this exercise, as far as the children were concerned, was
undoubtedly that where possible it is wise to check one's answer
against the facts provided, even if this checking takes a little more
time. In the second problem of this type, the only children who
offered the teacher a wrong solution were three who had not
checked for themselves; some took a longish time, but at least
they were able to correct the errors they discovered by personal
checking.

The second problem consisted of seven statements about which
day of the week it was. In this instance, six of the statements were
false. Most of the statements were indirect references to the actual
day and a solution was extremely difficult unless the individual
statements were put into a positive form saying what day each
claimed it to be. Some of the children spotted this need quite
quickly and soon produced correct solutions, which they had
checked. Others worked out a complicated series of statements
which brought them no nearer solution; it was only when these
attempts did not work out that they decided that there must be
an easier way, which they eventually found. They then tested
their solutions against the date, and showed great pleasure on
proving that they were correct.

These problems had a more favourable reception than those
involving numbers and so it was decided to go on to more difficult
closed system problems in the hope that the confidence which
was now being acquired by the majority of the children would help
them to successful solutions and a greater readiness to attack
unfamiliar questions. An example of the more complicated pro-

blem, taken from Emmet, required the children to use the data
provided to determine the professions and ages of four men.
Certain key facts were given but these led only part of the way
towards a solution, so that the would-be solver had to suspend his
judgement in much the same way as one is obliged to do in a
crossword puzzle, when one suspects that one knows a word but
wisely defers writing it in before checking two or three of the
letters by solving some other clues. Several partial solutions were
offered but the solvers had to be told that their solution was only
partly correct. It was demonstrated once again that most of these
bright children had become accustomed to solve the ordinary
school problem very quickly and were conditioned to the expectation that a quick look should produce the insight leading to an
answer. When they offered their erroneous or partly right solutions and were told that they must return to their desks for another
try, several showed impatience and annoyance; two or three children who were sent back for further effort for a second time showed
signs of extreme exasperation, approaching almost to despair. This
was the kind of humiliation to which most of these children were
completely unaccustomed. The first successes occurred among the
pupils, mainly boys, who, as a carry-over from previous problems,
made a table containing the certain data provided. This procedure did not cut down the amount of reasoning required, but it did
reduce the amount of apparently conflicting information to be
sorted out in one's head. Moreover these methodical children who
used a table tended also to check their solutions. They made no
attempt to rush them to the teacher so that they could claim to
be the first successful solvers. Ultimately, all the children adopted
the method of putting their data in tabular form, which helped
to show them or to pinpoint where their discrepancies lay. The
first correct solutions were presented after about ten minutes,
which was extremely good going for children, especially for those
of the younger groups. When two or three of them were invited
to explain their reasoning they tended to refer to their tables, and
on the whole they were able to give quite lucid explanations; none
tried to dispense with the tables.

Later in the course of the experiment, the groups were invited
to participate in a discussion in which an attempt was made to

assess the value of this introductory course. It was soon evident that some of the children remembered vividly, and in one or two cases almost poignantly, these early experiences. The prejudice against some of the number problems tended to persist, especially amongst the girls, but there was little sign of a similar prejudice against the other reasoning problems. A few of the bright children had realized at the time that there was a progression in the programme and that they had been learning new techniques, which they felt had been of benefit to them in their work generally. Amongst others, one small, young, very bright and very sensitive boy said that what he remembered most clearly was coming out for a second time on one of the problems, only to be told that he had still been unsuccessful. He could not recall when this had happened to him previously in school. One girl, perhaps a future pillar of the Women's Liberation Movement, asserted that she had felt so frustrated on one or two occasions that she had been on the verge of tears, but the thought that there were boys present, who seemed to be doing better than she was, helped her to restrain the tears and carry on to a successful solution. In the younger group in particular, some of the children maintained that at first there had been some loss of confidence in themselves and because of this they derived a certain feeling of resentment against the Queer Kids' course. However, once the initial shock had worn off and they found that with care and determination they could solve the problems set, their self-confidence returned and thereafter they were prepared to tackle whatever was set. There was no evidence that the children were making these statements because they thought they would please the experimenter: in one or two cases letters from the parents confirmed what the children had said.

At this point it should be made clear that the prejudice against problems involving numbers was very limited and at no time applied to the boys. Later in the experiment, some quite difficult number series were given to the groups, again taken from Emmet. In this instance, the children were invited to find as many number series as they could, given a list of numbers with one or two blanks in the columns. Most of the youngsters enjoyed doing this kind of exercise in which there seemed to be little pressure and prestige did not seem to be so intensely involved as in the early number problems. Indeed, some of the more out-of-the-way but perfectly defensible series were produced by the girls. In another instance a list of numbers was given, as, for example,

$$67 \quad 8442 \quad 2412 \quad 6030 \quad 5025 \quad 4422$$

and the children had to state what they had in common. Most of them found, by trial, that all the numbers were divisible by 67. The number 67 was then rubbed out and the children were invited to state what the remaining numbers had in common apart from divisibility by 67. It took a little time for them to notice that in each number the first pair is twice the second pair so that all the numbers are based on 201. When they were asked to find several four-figure numbers which would be divisible by 201, and so by 67, all the youngsters promptly proceeded to write down several examples. One felt that if all the boys and girls had begun number in the modern way, using a number line, perhaps they would not have shown the doubts and lack of confidence in their ability to handle numbers that they did display.

6

Intellectual Challenge

Although some of the bright children had shown a measure of success in dealing with some of the problems from Valentine's Higher Reasoning Test, these problems had proved too difficult for the majority and in some instances had affected confidence adversely. In one sense, of course, the reason for using such difficult material was to make the children realize that real-life problems rarely offered such limited procedures as did so many school problems with guaranteed neat answers and carefully prepared material. In that sense the purpose might be described as undermining a too simple confidence, which would be shattered as soon as more complex problems occurred, and building up in its place a stronger self-confidence structured on a much broader base and so more likely to withstand problems of greater difficulty or complexity. This proved to be, as might well have been expected, a rather delicate process calling for much more thought and finesse than it had received in earlier work. In consequence, it was decided not to make further use of the test itself until the children were older and more sure of themselves. This decision did not, however, preclude the use of the ideas underlying the problems set in that test, namely the presentation of problems with insufficient or with irrelevant information. With this end in view, two problems, which were believed to be easier, were devised and set to the children. The two problems were:

1 At 12.15 a shopkeeper heard a crash and noticed that his front window had been broken. He rushed out of the shop and caught a glimpse of a boy turning a nearby corner. He reported to the police that he thought that the boy was just

over 5 feet in height and that he was wearing a bright shirt or pullover and light-coloured shorts.

Jim was seen three-quarters of a mile away from the shop at 12.25. He was wearing a yellow football shirt and light grey shorts and carrying a football. His height is 5 feet 2 inches and he is about 12 years of age. When seen he seemed to have a worried look.

Tom was seen a quarter of a mile away from the shop at 12.19. He seemed to have been running. He was wearing school uniform consisting of a yellow pullover and light grey corduroy shorts. He was carrying a large stick with a big knob on top. He is about 12 years of age and just over 5 feet in height.

It is certain that the window was broken by one of these boys.

Below are six statements. Underline any of the statements which must be true. Put a question mark in the box on the right opposite any statement which *might* be true and put a cross opposite any statement which is not true.

1 Jim broke the window	
2 Jim could have broken the window	
3 Jim could not have broken the window	
4 Tom broke the window	
5 Tom could have broken the window	
6 Tom could not have broken the window	

2 In a family there are five children who receive pocket-money as follows:

Bill who is 18 and in form 6 has £1.20 a week.
Mary who is 16 and in form 5 has 85p a week
Janet who is 14 and in form 3 has 45p a week
Tom who is 13 and in form 2 has 30p a week
Peter who is 12 and in form 1 has 10p a week

On what principles are the amounts decided?

The first one, as with Valentine, gives an insufficiency of evidence to determine conclusively which of the boys was the culprit, and it is only when the youngsters have observed this fact that they can answer correctly the question about the statements in the table. If the children decided on the guilt of one of the boys as proved, then their answers would be wrong. As it turned out, the test as such was too easy for the older children of whom some 70 per cent had 6 marks out of 6, and all but one of the rest had 4 out of 6. The problem proved more difficult for the 10 to 11 group, in which just under 40 per cent had full marks and another 20 per cent had 4 out of 6. On further inquiry it was found that the younger children, on the whole, were more likely to conclude that one of the boys was almost certainly guilty, and so the statements were filled in to suit the theory. Most of the children subscribing to this view were, in fact, finding it hard not to play the part of detective, and in their experience detectives usually got their man. To check up on this, the problem was set again later on to another group, but without the statements. These younger children were invited to decide which boy was guilty and to give their reasons for this decision. No hint was given that there might be a third possible answer, because there was insufficient evidence. Some 40 per cent finally declared that they were unable to make up their minds because either of the boys could have broken the window. The other 60 per cent chose one boy, the favourite being the one with the football. Some of the boys had themselves had the experience of breaking a window with a football and so they were pretty certain of the culprit, and were surprised that so many of the other pupils could not spot him.

One or two of the brighter children in the earlier groups were not happy about the wording of the statements. When questioned more closely, during a discussion on the problem and its format, they found it difficult to justify their complaints but felt that the statements were somehow misleading. The one causing the most dissatisfaction was "Tom could not have broken the window." One of the children pointed out that although Tom was carrying a stick he was in school uniform and so readily identifiable. No boy in such a situation would run the risk of breaking a window in a public place. For this reason the statement must be true. Two other boys corroborated this claim, but whether they had just thought of it as they sought for a justification of an answer marked wrong, or whether they had actually reasoned on these lines it is impossible to say as it was a group discussion. This tendency to import into a situation or problem material from outside is not uncommon in people whose thought processes tend to be rather loose, but it is not necessarily a sign of loose thinking in the case of bright children. Time after time, the author has found that, after the most careful preparation and elaborate independent checking of number series and other tests which have apparently been rendered thoroughly closed, some gifted child has produced a completely unexpected answer or variation which has proved to be a correct answer or alternative. To put it another way, children and especially very bright children will provide unexpected answers sometimes acceptable sometimes not, because they give a question too much attention. Any teacher or would-be tester of such children must look twice at apparently wrong and out-of-the-way answers, to make sure that the actual reasoning is not of a higher nature than the test itself. On the other hand, no special sympathy was accorded to the boy who justified a wrong answer by assertin that the yellow jersey and light grey shorts was an absurd uniform: at the time of his assertion he was himself wearing a light-coloured pullover and light grey shorts.

The second problem reproduced here was an attempt to devise one which, like Valentine's, would require the elimination of an irrelevancy together with the need to compare certain related facts. This attempt was not very successful and as it turned out the problem was probably more difficult and complicated than the one which inspired it. Later experience showed that it would have been sufficient to give the ages and the classes with the amounts on the same rate for boys and girls. The unfairness of a lesser sum for the girls was far too difficult for the youngsters, who had had no previous experience of this type of problem and who did not think in the old-fashioned terms of different rates for the two sexes. It had been expected that the very bright children would compare the amounts given (*a*) to the three boys and (*b*) to the two girls, but in the actual working not a child attempted this, even after being given the hint that the problem contained an injustice to the girls.

In view of the weakness inherent in the problem and in view also of the fact that some 50 per cent of the children answered that there were no principles underlying the distribution (perhaps they were right, since the solution was devised, as for a detective story, before the rest of the problem) no mention would have been made in this report but for the varied reactions of the children. Several spent only a short time scrutinizing the problem and then decided that no solution was possible, and even when encouraged to try again, with the assurance that there were principles involved, they soon gave up. Others felt that they should be able to solve what appeared to them on the surface to be a simple problem involving the simplest of arthmetic. When the supervisor saw the difficulties experienced by the children, he suggested that comparing the top line and the bottom line (the oldest with the youngest) should be tried. Some did so, and one or two subtracted the bottom line from the top. They were now approaching a solution for the boys but none saw the possibility of comparing the new statement with the original top line which would have given them the answer for the boys. Some of the older children had had experience of simultaneous equations, but they were unable to apply their knowledge in this instance. Perhaps if the differing amounts for the boys and girls had been omitted some of the pupils would have solved the problem.

As some of the children had been successful, the problem was worked out for them on the blackboard and there were several interesting reactions. As a result all were agreed that it was possible to solve the problem, especially if one knew how it was made up. Several pointed to the unfairness of the different amounts for the girls, and thought that they might have been successful if the two primary principles of age and class had been the only ones. Two of the girls remarked that they were surprised now at how easy it seemed, but they had decided almost as soon as they had seen the problem that it was mathematical and so beyond their powers. One boy, a shrewd critic at all times, argued that this had been set as a test rather than as a problem. In ordinary school-work, he maintained, the teacher usually taught some new material in a lesson, after which the pupils were given some examples to do to show that they had understood the lesson and to give them

practice in the new work. This particular problem had been set
without any teaching beforehand: he was sure that if he had been
taught the necessary technique for tackling this problem he would
have solved it, or similar problems, quite easily. This assertion
was promptly put to the test and a similar problem was written
on the board, involving two principles only. All the children on
this occasion worked out the solution quickly and contentedly.
The group, together with the shrewd critic, at once made a remark
equivalent to "I told you so!" When a defence was offered that at
least some of the children had already experienced simultaneous
equations and so, in a sense, had the necessary technique, the
children concerned pointed out that in their Maths they had
learned to work on two equations, but in this particular problem
there had been no fewer than five statements, with nothing to
indicate that two should be taken at a time, the statements turned
into symbols and solutions worked out. Now that the proper
technique had been demonstrated to them, they could see that
application of their Maths lesson, and in future would be on the
alert when any such problem was set to them. They suggested that
in any similar situation in the future they should be warned that,
although the problem or material seemed to be outside their
previous experience, they might have the relevant information or
technique already as part of their knowledge derived from other
subjects. If no such warning were given, then they would be entitled to assume that it was a test of their intelligence and that
they must use their ingenuity to find a solution. This expression
of their opinions has been rendered more cogent than their views
actually were but despite their groping to make their views and
feelings clear, the author feels that his group provided a valuable
lesson for himself and for other educationists.

   Another of the techniques used to stimulate the children's
intelligence was the bringing into the schools of a number of
speakers from outside, or of sometimes inviting members of the
staff to speak. The first qualification of such speakers was that they
should have something interesting to say. On several occasions
when forthcoming engagements were announced the remark would
be passed, "Let's hope that he'll be interesting!" Strict relevance
to any of the subjects the children were studying was not absol-

utely necessary but there was usually more enthusiasm when the children were able to sense some relevance to a part of their exam-directed curriculum. On the whole it was an advantage if the speakers had had some experience of talking to audiences, prefer-ably adult audiences. Some of the people invited were accustomed to addressing adult audiences for commercial purposes: one or two of these inquired whether they should simplify their material and avoid technical terms. The answer to that query was that they should treat the children as an adult audience except for the fact that they were not trying to sell anything. Indeed there was a good chance that the average intelligence of the children would be higher than that of their more usual audiences. As far as technical terms were concerned, they should use them, but if they sensed that they were not being understood they should give the meaning as well. These very bright children tend to pick up such terms very quickly and if they have them explained they are adding to their knowledge.

Another query was about vocabulary generally. Some speakers felt that they would be uncomfortable and hesitant if they had to remind themselves from time to time that they were talking as they would normally do to educated people. To allay these doubts it was pointed out to the speakers that children, like adults, use vocabularies at different levels according to their circumstances. When they are with other children they use words which are acceptable to the other children, since if they did not conform to the norm of the group, they would soon find themselves excluded or even derided as "professors." On the other hand, where the parents are highly educated and the level of vocabulary at home is high, the speech of the home is very different from that of the playground group or even of the class. Anyone taking a class of very bright children for the first time or two will, if sensitive to different levels of vocabulary, soon notice that the level changes. Provided that a teacher uses his own extensive vocabulary freely, the children of ability will soon respond, or, if they have con-fidence in him, will ask about words with which they are unfamiliar. Once the speakers were reassured in this way, they usually carried on in their wonted style without further worry. All were asked to provide an opportunity for discussion, and it was usually during

this stage of the proceedings that they found themselves taken
aback by the quality of the children's questions.

A brief reference to some of the lecturers will serve to illustrate
their function. For example, one who spoke to the 12—13 + group
was a nutrition expert, Mr F. Edwards. His everyday job is giving
advice to farmers on the improvement of their stock and the
output of that stock. An enthusiast for his work, he carries this
enthusiasm into his speech and his approach to a topic. He made
use of a very helpful film which showed the function of the
rumen in the digestion of cattle. The film had been made for
adults and the vocabulary level was distinctly adult, but the children had no difficulty in following its teaching. They saw that
Mr Edwards was carrying out his promise, made in his introductory
remarks, to treat his audience as he did when he gave lectures to
groups of farmers. After the film the children were invited to ask
questions about it, or suggested by it. Several of the questions were
quite technical, as some of the children linked up the contents of
the film with what they had been learning in Biology, but they
soon passed on from the film to wider issues, such as the effect on
farming in the United Kingdom of Britain's decision to join the
Common Market. The one unfortunate fact was the lack of time,
as only one ordinary school period was available for our film and
discussion: the final bell of the afternoon rang just as the discussion
was becoming really involved.

Reactions were sought afterwards, first from the speaker and
subsequently from the children. The speaker, unused to an audience
of children, was a little uncertain as to whether he had performed
in a way useful to the children. Reassurance on that doubt could be
given without consulting the children, because it had been clear
to the author, as spectator, that all the children had watched the
film with interest. Also, the quality and range of the questions
had been largely of the kind one would expect from an adult
audience. The vocabulary had been at the level normal for specialist group work and well above the level normal for children of
their age. Most important of all, however, was the attitude of the
children towards the speaker. There was, quite naturally, the
respect shown by children in a good school towards visitors, but
there was in addition an acceptance of the speaker as one who was

willing to talk to them about his special subject and yet treat them as equals in the pursuit of knowledge. It is in an atmosphere of this type and quality that these youngsters show themselves at their best, and it is when this mutual respect exists between teacher and pupils that these very bright children are most likely to be challenged and to learn. Their response has its effect on the speaker, who tends to raise his own level: when this occurs there is a feeling of intellectual contact, which is sometimes followed, as more than one of our speakers said, by the feeling that virtue has gone out of one.

The children's reactions, which could not be ascertained immediately, were wholly favourable. The subject had proved interesting but it had had the added attraction that it linked up to some extent with part of their ordinary school-work. Only one boy suggested that it might help him ultimately in his "O" level exam. They had all enjoyed the film and hoped that later speakers might also make use of films. After a little probing, some reactions to the speaker himself were forthcoming. One of these was that he obviously knew his subject thoroughly and so was able to answer any of the questions raised. Another was that he was obviously a clever man and so it was a pleasure to ask him questions and to obtain his views on the current controversy about Britain entering the Common Market. Finally, one of the girls remarked that she had felt that the speaker treated the group as if they were as intelligent as himself and that this had made her try harder to take part. Most of the others agreed that it had been refreshing not to be patronized: they did not, of course, use that term.

An outside lecture of a somewhat similar type was tried with the 11—12-year old group. On this occasion the subject was the processing of peat, which seemed appropriate as the school stands quite near the centre of the Somerset peat trade: peat is cut, processed and exported mainly for horticultural purposes to various other parts of the country. The speaker, Mr N. Grainger, had worked in the peat business for several years and had undergone a course of training in lecturing on the subject. Apart from some samples of peat at various stages of processing, his equipment consisted of a flow-chart illustrating the process from beginning to

end. The children, of course, constituted an unusually young
audience for one accustomed to addressing adults: the group
consisted also of children of high or very high IQ. For them, too,
it was a new experience. No one from industry or trade had come
to talk to them before. Most of them came from a considerable
distance away from the peat area so that the subject was entirely
new to them. Three of them came from farming communities and
this fact showed up in the questioning of the speaker, who worked
from the flow-chart and who broke up his lecture into three parts
with an opportunity for questions after each part.

As in the example already given, there were three noticeable
points. The first of these was the speed with which the speaker settled
down to work with an audience which showed the normal courtesy
and an immediate interest. When he had completed his first section
he found that questions flowed readily and that they were apposite
and on occasion searching. Fortunately, he was ready for all of
them, and so he settled down quickly to his second section. He
mentioned afterwards that by this time he had completely rid
himself of any qualms that he might have had, and he had pretty
well forgotten that he was dealing with an audience of relatively
young children. When an opportunity was given to study the
samples further questions were invited. The second feature was
the consistently high standard of the questions, some of which
concerned the flow-chart. "Was it drawn to scale?" was one such
question. Several were about what happened if something went
wrong in the process. Such questions gave the speaker the chance
to outline alternative routes in the process and also certain safe-
guards built into the system. One girl, daughter of a farmer, compared parts of the process with certain mechanical processes used
on the farm at home. This girl, who had often shown a great deal
of commonsense and also an impatience with, or lack of interest
in, some of the personality queries and discussions, manifested an
interest previously dormant and played a most stimulating part
in the period-activity. The third feature was again the nature of
the response, which was one of genuine interest and engagement.
One boy expressed his view afterwards, declaring that the speaker
seemed to treat them as intelligent beings and on a level with himself. Another pupil, a girl, who sometimes seemed to feel relief

when the lesson came to an end, confessed that for once she was sorry to hear the signal for the end of the period.

Another such successful period with the 13—14-year-old group was contributed by the Careers master, but that one will be dealt with in Chapter 9, under the heading of "Self-understanding." On the whole it seemed better to obtain speakers from outside the school itself, since they would not be associated with school in the minds of the children. On the other hand, it is unwise not to make use of the pool of ability which is to be found in a school staff of any size. All too often those arranging stimulating programmes in a school are unaware of any of the outside interests of the various members of the staff. A statement of these interests may have appeared on the application forms of teachers when they were seeking their jobs, but after that the emphasis is often on the academic or sporting specialisms. Teachers themselves often make no mention of some useful experience or hobby. Some of the problems of providing stimulation for a very bright child might well be found in a canvass of the staff to discover interests which might be utilized. Teachers who have something of this nature to offer might well, should circumstances permit, be given the chance to join any programme, whether intra- or extra-curricular. This might prove to be an easier solution than finding suitable outside speakers, who may not have had the experience of talking to or stimulating activities with groups of children. From experience, and from the remarks of the very bright children at different times, one could, I believe, say that the attitude and group-management of the speakers are at least as important as the content of the lecture. One 12-year-old summed the matter up as well as anybody could when he declared after a talk that the speaker had made him think in a way that irritated him at first, but in the end he felt that he had enjoyed himself more than in some of the other talks in which he had agreed all the time with what was being said.

Another lecture which brought both favourable reactions and responses was one given by another of the Millfield staff, Mr A. Sparrow, on the uses and abuses of Statistics. Most of the children in the group had already been introduced to such terms as mean, median and standard deviation, in relation to some of the tests they had sat, with especial reference to their scores on the AH4.

The lecture was not concerned with such technical details but it seemed to the children to be linked with other aspects of their school-work and so a favourable atmosphere pre-existed. There was some measure of scepticism as most of the youngsters were familiar with the pronouncement that there are lies, damned lies and statistics. Indeed, perhaps the most remarkable feature of the response was the obvious awareness of the group of the invalid use of numbers in the alleged statistical bases for advertisements. While they appreciated such uses as sampling traffic conditions for the purpose of considering where a new relief road might most advantageously be built, or on a housing estate to ascertain how many new school places were required, they produced more examples of the possible misuses, when the speaker came to discuss and illustrate these. Some made reference to advertisements in commercial television which used statistics in a doubtful way, and one or two others quoted what they regarded as misuses by politicians. There was some discussion about the use made of samples of reactions to programmes on the mass media; doubts were expressed about the extrapolation to millions of viewers from an apparently small sample. The idea of random numbers appealed to some, but it was agreed that the use of these might not be justified, except perhaps in cases of redistribution of wealth by such media as ERNIE. It was interesting to note that while most of the children played some part in the questioning and discussion, two very recent very bright recruits to the group seemed to be in their element in this type of study. These boys, with one or two others including the best mathematician in the group, seemed very much at home in dealing with graphs and the misuse of them. They were clearly already on their guard against the misleading types of graphs and histograms so frequently used in advertisements and in certain political pamphlets, and it looked as if the children who were less experienced in this particular field had been awakened to some of the dangers arising from abuse, whether deliberate or resulting from ignorance. This certainly proved to be a most useful form of mental stimulation for a group of 13—14-year-olds.

7

Discussions

Teachers have favoured discussions as a means of stimulating children orally, but many of these have been restricted in value, largely because, in relatively large classes, they tend to be dominated by those who are already able to speak in front of an audience even when they may have little that is worth while to say. The shy children, even if interested in the topic, on which they may possess some useful and thoughtful views, are likely to hesitate and to sit back in the shadow of the readier speakers. This difficulty did not apply, in the oral sessions, to the groups at Millfield and Edgarley, but all the groups included in the experiment contained children who were much more fluent on paper than in speech in front of others. Consequently, there was still the need to make sure that these children made a reasonable contribution and that they obtained as much practice in the art of addressing and interesting an audience as was possible. Such contributions as "I agree with the last speaker," without some further personal idea, were not acceptable, even if occasionally it proved necessary for the person in charge of the discussion to help out with appropriate questions.

The second common difficulty in stimulating a worthwhile discussion is obviously the choice of a suitable topic. This must provoke thought and yet not be so remote from the interest of the children that they find it difficult to speak freely on the subject. On the other hand, many topics are so commonplace or so familiar to the children that they lead to the most banal expressions of views and are more likely to cause boredom or lack of interest than to stimulate intellectual effort. If this is applicable to children of average, or just above average ability, it is very much more so to children of high intellectual ability. This fact and some others will now be illustrated from accounts of four of the discussions, one with a Millfield group and the other three with one of the Edgarley sub-groups.

The first of these discussions was on the raising of the school-leaving age and took place at a time when there had been strong criticism of the Government's determination to press ahead with the raising of the age to 16 in the United Kingdom. Almost at the same time, an American educationist visiting this country had stated publicly that Britain should be following some of the States and raising the leaving age to 18. Circumstances seemed favourable for a discussion, but, as most of the children were used to the idea of staying at school to the age of 18, it was felt that it would be more fitting to choose the statement of the American as the basis of the discussion. A few minutes were given to preparation, after the children had been reminded that there were usually arguments available on both sides of a proposal. They made brief notes and then were invited to express their views. All, eventually, had an opportunity to express themselves, but for the most part all the ideas expressed had already been disclosed by the end of the second contribution. Each speaker in turn produced one or two reasons for raising the the age and one or two difficulties which might apply to children who wished to leave school before the age of 18. Except for two pupils who had already begun a tentative questioning of the so-called joys and benefits of "the happiest years of our lives," all were agreed that 18 was the right age for themselves and for many other children in the country. There was some understanding that some children disliked school and derived little benefit from it: such children would be happier and better off at work, provided suitable work was obtainable. But apart from the two dissidents there was no sign of any empathic feeling for, or understanding of, the children whose schooling was in very different circumstances from their own. Even the dissidents, a boy and a girl, although they claimed that there were more arguments for retaining the leaving age of 15 than for raising it to 18, showed little thought for children with unfavourable homes and poor schools. They themselves felt tired of school and were actually challenging some of the traditional school values, but they did not make any real effort to put themselves in the place of others.

This discussion proved disappointing. It never developed into a proper discussion but remained a symposium in which each person made a reasonable and reasoned contribution. The temperature remained low throughout and none of the statements brought any reaction indicative of emotion or feeling. The contributors were almost exclusively concerned with themselves, and as school life was their norm they failed to look at the question from any viewpoint other than their own. No one raised any of the problems status that might arise from "school-children" of 18 calling at the polling station on their way to school, to vote as adults; when they were asked what they thought of this as a way of spending a school period, the general opinion was that it would be "all right!" but there was no sign of any enthusiasm or any request for further discussion. When one boy was asked if he thought that more interesting and stimulating points could have been debated, he reflected for a minute and then said, "I shall be staying at school till I'm 18 in any case, so it did not seem to affect me very much, but if you had suggested that we should all stay at school till we were 20, I'd have had a lot more to say."

Another discussion which it was hoped would lead to intellectual stimulation and perhaps to emphatic understanding, was based on one which had provided one or two remarkable contributions when used with the first very bright children to come to Brentwood. This was the story taken from Plato's *Crito*, concerning the offer of the friends of Socrates to help him escape from prison. While Socrates expresses appreciation of the thoughtfulness of his friends in proposing that he should exchange clothes with one of them and slip out of prison, he insists that he cannot avail himself of their offer, since he would be running away, thus breaking the law which he had spent his life supporting. At Brentwood, where the group of children had been about 9+ years of age, the story had sparked off a very interesting discussion with the majority taking the Socratic standpoint, while a small minority of boys decided that it would be foolish to wait quietly to be put to death when it was avoidable, even if it meant a form of exile. On that occasion, a question which seemed just to emerge from the discussion was, "Is there anyone from whom you cannot escape?"

The first reply, from several of the children, was "God." When the question was repeated, one boy rather hesitantly suggested, "Oneself!" Before long, several of the children agreed with this answer. Then another question was propounded: "Where can we sometimes meet people who seemed to have escaped from themselves?" Almost immediately, the boy who had answered "Oneself," but this time without a trace of hesitation, said "In a lunatic asylum." Another boy then corrected this to "a mental hospital." It was obvious, if surprising, that one or two of these 9—10-year-olds had already thought about such matters.

It was assumed that this topic would bring something still more remarkable from a group of children some three years older than the Brentwood children. This time, most of the children had heard of Socrates, but this seemed hardly to be an advantage, as there were clearly no hero-worshippers in the group. A few had heard the story from the *Crito*, but had never thought about its meaning or its implication; it tended to remain just something you heard about in school, and therefore of no great significance. Although there were several boys in the group who were quite likely to be "agin' the law," almost all the children quickly agreed that Socrates was right to remain in prison. When an attempt was made to probe the subject further, one or two children pointed out that it was difficult to come to any other conclusion since we already knew the outcome of the affair and that even if they demanded otherwise, it was not going to affect an issue settled well over 2,000 years ago. A further attempt to guide the children into the same sort of discussion as at Brentwood, about the possibility of escaping from oneself, called forth some appreciation of the point but little of the intellectual excitement which had been stirred up at Brentwood. The next step was to ask the children to approach the story in a different way and to analyse two questions: firstly, if you had been one of the friends visiting Socrates in prison, what advice would you have given him? And secondly, if one of your own friends were in prison at the present time, and the opportunity occurred to help him to escape, what would you do? They were invited to spend a little time thinking out the issues involved; thoughtful answers were required, so they should not blurt out the first idea coming into their minds.

The result was a much more dynamic and interesting discussion. The first question, about the decision facing Socrates' friends, was taken first. Again, the majority of the children agreed that they would have put forward the arguments advanced by the previous friends: they felt they would have stressed that it would be foolish for such an outstanding man to be killed, so that other people would be denied, unnecessarily, the benefit of his wisdom. On the whole, however, they were doubtful if their arguments would have been powerful enough to persuade Socrates to change his mind. It was, perhaps, significant that two or three said that now, having looked at the problem from another point of view, they had begun to appreciate Socrates' attitude much more than when they had simply agreed with it at the beginning of the discussion. It became clear that with this group at least this would have been a more stimulating approach than the more direct one used. Passing on to the second question, concerning one of their own friends, the discussion became much more animated and the degree of disagreement much wider. One or two strayed away from the actual problem to the much more congenial contemplation of methods which might be used by them in effecting the escape. Others maintained that their decision would depend on what crime or offence their friend had been imprisoned for. If it were a very serious crime, then they might no longer regard the prisoner as a friend. If it were, in their view, a minor matter such as some offence connected with civil liberties or with contempt of court, then they would advise their friend to attempt an escape and they would do their utmost to render the attempt successful. When time brought the discussion to an indecisive end, most of the group felt that they had enjoyed the second part of it and proposed that further discussions of problems with which they might find themselves confronted should be included from time to time in the programme.

The third discussion was based on the useful educational principle, which will be referred to again under the heading of creativity, that the familiar should be made to look unfamiliar at least as often as one decides to proceed from the familiar to the unfamiliar. Children tend to be conditioned, or else to condition themselves to the familiar relationship of pupil to teacher, so that they find it difficult to revise their view of the relationship. In view of this tendency, one of the groups was presented with the following situation: it was explained to them that four persons had looked through the window into a class-room in a school and thereafter each had made a statement.

Person A had said "I see 20 children and an adult"
    " B "   " "I see 20 pupils and a teacher"
    " C "   ,, "I see 21 learners"
    " D "   " "I see 21 teachers"

The first reaction to statements C and D was to regard them as nonsensical, and so it was proposed that each statement should be discussed in turn. Even so, some of the children thought that A and B should be regarded as synonymous until it was pointed out to them by others in the group that the adult in the class-room might not be a teacher but only someone temporarily in charge of the children. One boy suggested that the children in A might not be school-children at all, whereas in B they were pupils, and so school-children. It was also suggested and generally agreed that the adult in A was not, in all probability, a teacher, otherwise the observer would have been expected to assume that the class-room contained a class being taught by a teacher. Statement B was accepted as sensible and normal, but one or two argued that it was not really informative. They wanted more information about the pupils (were they boys or girls or both; were they Infant, Junior or Secondary school children?) When the group was asked whether the pupils might not be adults in an evening class, they quickly pointed out that A's statement ruled out that possibility. They agreed that statements of C and D were of little help in trying to answer this question. One girl thought that the statements should be left separate.

When the group passed on to Statement C, there were some difficulties until it was suggested that, while the pupils were obviously learners in the current class-room situation and the teacher was not, the teacher must be studying outside the class-room, perhaps for another qualification. This solution seemed to please the majority for the time being, but not all the children were satisfied. One of the youngest and by nature most argumentative remarked that they were doing what they had been consistently told in the group not to do, namely, importing outside ideas into the statement. This referred to the class-room situation visible through the window and the sense or absurdity of the statement must be determined within the limits of the situation. This argument, cogently and lucidly expressed, brought about a reconsideration of the statement and led to most of the group breaking away from the orthodox viewpoint. They then began to see that a teacher in a class-room is a learner, at least in so far as he acquires information about the children and about their performance and capabilities. They freely admitted that they had not thought of teachers in this light previously. In the next minute or two, other ideas were put forward about what a teacher could learn from his pupils; gradually they began to realize that teachers can indeed learn from pupils, whose combined store of knowledge is greater than that of any single adult can be. All were eventually obliged to agree that the statement was at least as sensible and acceptable as A and B.

Despite this agreement, no one applied the idea immediately to statement D, when the group passed on to consider it. Twenty-one learners, yes, but twenty-one teachers, no! Presently, one youngster saw the light in one respect, and excitedly remembered that if the teacher learned from the children then that was the same as saying that the children were able to teach the teacher something. In that sense, at times all 21 persons were teachers. The group seemed ready to accept this and assumed that there was nothing further to add. When prodded a little about their complacency, they began to consider the situation afresh and soon one bright spark saw that if people work and play together they must have opportunities to learn from each other. No one had thought of this during the discussion on statement C, because all had been much too preoccupied with the idea of the teacher as one of the 21 learners. Now they could see that in this sense every member of a group or class was a teacher and that teaching itself could take many forms. They began to give examples of teaching which they had not formerly regarded as teaching. They quoted cases where they had asked other children to explain some point which they had found difficult: one boy said that often, when he asked another boy or girl to show him how to do something, he would think to himself, "What I am really saying to this person is 'please teach me how to do this'."

After this apparent break-through from the familiar viewpoint to an unfamiliar way of regarding a commonplace situation, two further questions were put to the children. These were:

1 Can you now reconcile the four statements?
2 Can you deduce anything else about learning and teaching from statement D?

All the children were now agreed that all four statements, applied to the situation seen through the window, could in fact be regarded as true and relevant: they were in the end merely four ways of looking at the same situation. All said that from now on they would look more carefully at statements which seemed at first sight nonsensical. The opportunity was then taken to explain what is meant by a paradoxical statement. The outcome of the discussion seemed eminently satisfactory, but the children did not rise to the occasion presented by question 2. Despite coaxing and prodding, no one was able to come up with the suggestion that teaching and learning are very closely related and that in fact teaching cannot, in many cases, be regarded as having taken place if there is no consequent learning. Nor was anyone able to see the possibility that learning is, in a sense, a case of teaching oneself. This was too much, obviously, to expect from children of 10+ to 11+, even although several had maximum scores on an IQ test. Nevertheless, it was one of the most profitable discussions.

A discussion on the meaning of an Intelligence Quotient was introduced and subsequently used with successive groups, because some of the children asked about their IQ. Many of them had been subjected to an Intelligence Test: some had been referred to an educational psychologist who had applied such a test, usually the Terman—Merrill 1960 revision, or the WISC. Others had been given a group test of the type produced by the NFER or Moray House. Most of the children had not realized that they were sitting an intelligence test and several had only a vague memory of the occasion. The majority had not been told the result of the test but a few appreciated that they had been sent to Edgarley somehow in consequence of the test. On the other hand, some children, for one reason or another, were aware of what their score had been and realized that they had put up an exceptional performance. Not all of these, however, had any real inkling of what an IQ meant and there was little evidence of any of the children going round informing others that they were high IQ children. They had their own system of appraisal and when a high IQ was mentioned, in the course of any discussion, they would sometimes suggest the names of those children whose preferences seemed to indicate a high IQ. It was interesting to note that their appraisal was sometimes widely different from that provided by the Intelligence Tests. One reason, therefore, for a discussion on IQ and tests was to clarify the ideas of the children.

By the second year of the experiment, all of the children had sat the AH4 test, and some of them had been submitted to it again. This provided a good starting point, since it was possible to begin with a number of scores which showed that most of those sitting the test a second time did considerably better. When the children were invited to explain this fact, some suggested that any test was easier a second time because people tended to remember parts of it. Most of the children who had sat the test twice assured the others that, although they had a vague recollection of the type of test it was, they had not remembered any of the items. They were then asked whether the AH4 test had been treated in exactly the same way as their ordinary class tests, when their teachers were trying to discover whether they had mastered the work of the last few days or weeks. At first there was some hesitation; then a boy declared that there was at least one difference. After a class test they usually received their papers back and so were able to see which items had been marked correct and which wrong. Indeed, sometimes the teacher would go over the questions and answers so that the children learned how to do those items in which they had previously made mistakes. After the AH4 they had not even been given their scores and had felt very little interest. They had not been told which items were right and they had not been taught how to correct any errors. The group now saw that the repetition of a test which had been taken under those conditions, a year ago, would not greatly help pupils sitting it for a second time. The consensus of opinion was that as most of the children had improved their scores, the improvement must be connected with their increase in age or else their increase of knowledge. It was pointed out that some of them had shown a much greater improvement than others: for example, one boy had a score of 67 one year and 98 the next. Was there any explanation of such an occurrence? Had the boy suddenly become much cleverer, whereas the other children had moved up by only a few points? After some uncertainty the group seemed to decide that probably the first score had been too low for some reason. Pressed for reasons, they were temporarily at a loss, but then good ideas began to flow. It was suggested that perhaps the boy had not been feeling well on the first occasion and that he was much fitter on the second. Perhaps he had had a toothache or perhaps he had received bad news. Perhaps one of his pets had been ill or had died. All could recollect exams or tests in which they had not done very well because they had been feeling tired or unwell or worried. They came to a unanimous conclusion that the state of one's health or one's mind could adversely affect the result of an exam. With a little guidance, they reached the further conclusion that it would be unfair to judge a person on one performance only, and that even in an intelligence test a person should sit at least twice, preferably with an interval between, before being placed in a certain category.

As the AH4 does not provide an IQ, but gives categories according to the scores and ages of the examinees, the discussion was still some distance from the subject of the IQ itself, but was on the threshold, as it was now possible to talk about norms. In the Manual, the nearest norms to the children were those of 14-year-old Grammar School children and it was possible to allow them to compare their own scores with these norms, reminding them that they were for children two or three years older than themselves. Most of them were rather pleased with the comparison and had every reason to be so.

While they were pleased with their AH4 scores, they had not yet had an explanation of an Intelligence Quotient. Some simple background information was given about the origin of Intelligence Tests, as for example about the problem created by the introduction of compulsory schooling for all children between certain ages. The Edgarley and Millfield children could see that if all children were made to attend school, then those who were not very clever would have to be taught as skilfully as the others. Some of the Western governments had been concerned about the number of children failing in school, and so the French government asked Professor Binet to examine the problem. He had accepted the idea that there were differences between children in personality and environment and so he had decided that he would try to devise tests which would show whether a child was subnormal in some ways. Out of this desire to find which children were backward had come the Intelligence Tests which, after some revisions, some of the children in the group had sat. They showed interest in the methods of Binet and his colleagues in finding what seemed to be a reasonable level of performance for each succeeding chronological age, so providing a mental age. As the chronological ages were known from the register, there was a possibility of comparing the so-called mental age with the chronological age. It was explained that the mental age depended on a score on an intelligence test compared with a norm for that test. The derivation of the IQ was then shown. Since it was possible to give an IQ score for a child below normal, it was obvious that it was possible also to give one for a child above normal. Reference was also made to the normal curve and to the use of standard deviation, but on the whole notions of dispersion did not greatly appeal to the younger children. Some of the older ones had already learned about standard deviation in their Maths.

One or two of the children wondered whether the IQ could change. This led to a discussion on what an IQ was and it was finally agreed that it was a ratio and that if the mean and deviation grew equally the ratio would be the same. They asked what the chances were that this would happen if the children were tested again, and were told that the changes did take place for a variety of reasons, but that it was rare for big changes to occur unless there were special reasons for a depressed score on one of the test occasions. This seemed to offer a good opportunity for discussing the concept of reliability, but it had been noticeable that the interest of the majority of the children in the subject was rapidly waning; even the 13+ pupils seemed to feel that this was an arid topic.

It was felt that it would be useful to give a simple introduction to some research ideas, to stimulate intellectual interest, especially as the children seemed to have only the vaguest notions of the meaning of the word. A few claimed to have undertaken some research, but further inquiry elicited the information that they had participated at some time in a "project" at school, or else they had been sent to the library to consult works of reference. Some other children mentioned that they had used for a time one of the "Finding Out" series of books. This revelation offered a good starting point and they were asked if they would like to see copies of an Attitudes Test which had actually been used as a basis of a piece of psychological and social research. All thought it a good idea. At one time, in Africa, the author made a study of the attitudes of a number of African school children and training college students, mostly boys of about 13 to 20+ years. The purpose was to gain some knowledge of the background of the children's lives and of how it affected their ambitions and desires and learning in school or college. Parts of the test were as follows:

SECTION ONE

Name. . . . .   Age. . . . .

Read the following and answer the questions

A Musa said to Audu and Umaru: "I hear that Oba has been very rude to his grandfather. I think that his father should beat Oba even if he is 17 years of age."

"No," said Umaru, "we must refuse to talk to Oba." Audu said: "There is no need for Oba to be punished now. His grandfather will soon be dead and then his spirit will cause Oba a great deal of trouble."

(*a*) With whom do you agree — Musa, Umaru or Audu? *Ans.*

(*b*) which is the severest punishment of these three? *Ans.*

B Shehu, Musa and Audu were talking together. Shehu said: "The teacher has found out that Aremu has been telling lies to him." Musa said: "The teacher should beat Aremu." Audu said: "Aremu should be sent away from school." Shehu said:

"He should be given a warning this time but not punished."
  (*a*) With whom do you agree — Shehu, Audu or Musa? *Ans.*
  (*b*) Are you sometimes beaten
      (1) at school? *Ans.*   (2) at home? *Ans.*

C Mamman said: "Ibrahim is looking very unhappy. I think he is feeling ill." Abubakar said: "He is not really ill. But last week an old woman (witch) told him that he would soon be ill if he stayed at school." Mamman said: "I do not believe that would make Ibrahim unhappy and look ill."
  (*a*) Could Abubakar's explanation be correct? *Ans.*
  (*b*) Could a witch make you (1) feel unhappy? *Ans.*
      and (2) feel ill? *Ans.*

SECTION TWO

Several friends were talking together and they made different statements. You will, no doubt, agree with some and disagree with others. If you strongly agree with any statement write a 3 after it: if you agree but not strongly write a 2 after it: if you are not sure whether you agree or not write a 1 after it: if you disagree with any statement write 0 after it.

  5 I feel that I am fully grown up
  7 I feel that I am a big boy but not an adult
  8 I feel that I am still a small boy
 10 My father still treats me as a child
 13 I feel that girls admire me
 16 Teachers treat me still as a child
 18 I like being told what to do
 21 My parents would like me to marry now
 22 I feel too young to marry yet
 30 Boys are usually cleverer than girls
 33 Several things worry me
 34 Girls do not need schooling

Blank copies of this attitude test were distributed to the Millfield and Edgarley children, and after they had read it through once they were invited to concentrate first of all on Section A.

They were asked why they thought that in A to D the form of a conversation had been used, followed by questions. Some young-sters decided that this particular form was chosen because it would prove interesting to the children answering. Others thought a dif-ferent form could have been equally interesting. In the end, a boy suggested that the technique seemed to be partly indirect and partly direct: the first question in each case was really asking about the views of somebody else, whereas the second question was seek-ing a personal view. On reflection, the rest of the group accepted this, and so it was possible to look more closely at the reason for using this technique, since it was obviously deliberate. One girl put forward the view, quite tentatively, that perhaps this method was devised to try to obtain truthful answers, whereas direct question-ing might have brought forth less truthful ones. It was now an appropriate time to explain to the children that the admission to school or college often depended on interviews, and it was important, in a country where educational opportunities were very restricted, that at such interviews candidates should give acceptable answers. They tended, therefore, to give the answers they felt the interviewers were seeking. Some African children had had to face several interviews and had become almost experts in giving suitable answers. Such answers would have been of little value in building up a true picture of their background, and so the help that they required would have been much more difficult to recognize and subsequently to provide.

Some children in the groups expressed doubts about the actual questions. They clearly found it hard to accept that adolescents would believe in the power of the spirits of the dead or the effects of a witch-doctor's arts on another person. A number of comple-ted forms were available and were shown to the children, after which a summary of the answers was drawn up. This revealed that almost a third of the sample accepted the haunting by the grand-father's spirit as the severest punishment, while a quarter thought they could be made unhappy or ill by a curse laid upon them. A few answers disagreed about the effect of the prophecy of the witch, but still accepted that they themselves might be affected. With a little questioning it was possible to guide the Edgarley children to the conclusion that this sort of belief still existed but in some cases at least there was a certain amount of confusion in the minds of the boys who had filled in the forms.

When the Edgarley children were asked what they had learned from their study of the first section, they listed three points on which there seemed to be a wide measure of agreement. Firstly, they had learned that even a questionnaire used in research may not be straightforward and that if it were to be of any real value it must be thought out carefully. A return to this was made in the consideration of the second part, as will be seen below. A second point was that the person making up a test of this sort would have to be careful to avoid letting the candidate know his own views, or that would be all he would get back from his test. A third point was that quite obviously people can still entertain seriously views which others have discarded: people who no longer hold certain views, which science seems to have disproved, claim that those who still believe them are superstitious. An attempt was then made to lead the children to the realization that to call some things superstitious is not really helpful, and that we should try to seek the reasons for the development and maintenance of a belief. This was of great importance in our dealings with immigrants into a country.

As the discussion arising from the study of the first part of the questionnaire seemed to have stimulated the children, a further study was made of the second part, of which a few examples are quoted on page 93. In this section these bright children soon began to realize that there were some statements which were more important than others from the point of view of the person devising the list. Once one of the boys had obtained confirmation from the author that this was so, the group set out in the manner of Sherlock Holmes to discover which were the most important statements. This activity led to another interesting period.

One of the groups taking part in this activity had previously undergone several personality inventories and projective techniques. the children in this group were invited, after studying the two parts, to write down what they considered to be the most valuable outcome for themselves of this brief study of a research technique. It was expected that most of the group would agree that they had learned a little about one meaning of the word "research." Actually, the answers of about half of the group could be summed up in the words of one of the girls: "If you are going to undertake a piece of research work you must think out carefully beforehand what you wish to learn and how you are going to obtain the information." Two or three of the other children were substantially agreed that the most important factor in some kinds of research is being able to persuade people to give "true" answers and not those which they think the tester wants them to give.

Finally, there was the conclusion of S. (a boy with a WISC maximum score) who wrote:

> The most important lesson I have learned is that in many of the tests and exercises which we have sat this technique had been used on us. We too have been asked all sorts of questions, some important and some not so. In other words we have been tricked just like the Africans

When this conclusion was read out to the group, all seemed to agree, and one girl expressed the views of the group when she remarked in not too unfriendly tones: "We shall be on our guard the next time."

8

Creativity

As was indicated in Chapter 1, the Millfield and Edgarley children
were chosen partly on the results of Creativity tests, but it is
perhaps significant that while the whole Edgarley school sat the
AH4 only a limited number were given the Creativity tests other
than the essays with the divergent titles, which all the children
had to write. One of the reasons for the much smaller number who
sat the Torrance tests was the difficulty in scoring them in a meaningful way; another was the amount of time required, and the test
time was always restricted by the regular demands of the school
timetable. Insufficient children sat the Creativity tests for us to
attempt any worthwhile correlations but such results as we did
have seemed to correspond roughly with the findings of Hudson
that more than a third of the children showed up well in both the
Creativity and Intelligence tests and that a little under a third
showed up better in one or other of the series of tests.

The fact that a considerable number of children did well in
both Intelligence and Creativity tests led to the bringing together
of Creativity and Intelligence rather than relating the Creativity
to the other aspects of this study, namely self-understanding and
the understanding of external relationships. There were other
reasons for this approach, one being that since Creativity was
isolated with a fair amount of success as a gift or quality in its
own right, a number of the test items which were formerly included in Intelligence tests are now regarded as indicative of Creativity.
At one time it was considered that the ability to perceive relationships, especially the less obvious ones, was a criterion of Intelligence: now, much of this kind of perception is regarded as one of
the bases of Creativity. The ability to perceive the familiar in an

unfamiliar way is accepted as a form of Creativity linked with novelty or originality and a good deal of literature seems to be the product of this relatively rare ability. But many of the children, and adults too, who have this particular gift are equally endowed with the ability to perceive and appreciate the more orthodox relationships such as Synonyms, Antonyms and Analogies which are still included in Intelligence tests.

Some of the limitations and difficulties which have already been described in connection with the attempts at intellectual stimulation applied to the Creativity tests, but on the whole the conditions for Creativity were more difficult than for the other categories. Common to both were the restrictions arising from the extreme shortage of time available and the physical limitations of space. Normally only one small class-room was available, and while with Marlowe we might rejoice at "Infinite riches in a little room," the methods usable were largely dictated by the physical conditions. This was of lesser importance in the case of the intellectual activities in which the test could be carried out or the relatively simple activities performed in a limited space. In Creativity, any activity requiring movement was not feasible. There was, however, still another limitation arising from the fact that the children were already officially engaging in creative work in several of the subjects on the timetable. Our activities had to be different from those of the regular classes.

In the case of the Intelligence test, usually the motivation was simple: the activities could be presented as a challenge, and with bright children this is adequate provided that the challenge involved is genuine. With the Creativity activities, the problem of motivation was much more complicated. Most of the Creativity tests which have been devised so far have resembled group Intelligence tests and so have been set under the same conditions as are to be found in any classroom when a "test" is set. This approach has been adversely criticized by Kogan and Wallach who maintain, in their *Modes of Thinking in Young Children*, that Creativity tests should be individual tests and that there is no need to urge children to produce creative work. Unfortunately, there is rarely a sufficiency of time to test children individually when numbers of children are involved and so there is no real alternative to the group test procedure. But even here there is a problem. Does one urge the children to write as interestingly as possible or as creatively as they can, thus underlining what the tester is searching for? Or does one simply present the material and tell the pupils to go on writing or composing or drawing, or what you will, until a signal is given to stop work? At Brentwood College of Education the completely unmotivated exercises had usually a banality about them which indicated a lack of interest or even boredom on the part of the children: the reader of their efforts was also likely to be bored.

At Millfield and Edgarley two of the Brentwood exercises were repeated without any invitation to be creative or interesting but in other cases material was provided which was assumed to be interesting in itself and the remark was made in these cases that the tester was looking forward eagerly to reading the interesting stories which they were about to write. This deliberate motivation seemed to have a favourable outcome in a number of cases but the general conclusion must be that the result was indecisive. This seems to be an area in which research is urgently required.

One of the Brentwood exercises which was repeated consisted of five groups of words which were not obviously linked. For example:

car, medicine, ring, knife
shop, sky, sand, people

An example was given but it was not particularly stimulating. The children were invited to make up little stories including each word but there was no directive that they should write interesting stories. The exercise proved a reasonably satisfactory stimulus for a small minority and was slightly more successful with the girls than with the boys. On the whole, however, it was treated as just another school exercise and so came under the rules of the stint. Even without the stint, however, it is doubtful if it would have stimulated the children to reveal anything of themselves. One of the most significant outcomes was the difficulty the exercise presented to a few of the boys, who found it extraordinarily hard even to start writing; and even when they did produce something it had little sign of creativity or fluency. It had become crystal-clear that other stimuli must be tried out and the next step was to use two forms of Story Completion. One of these had already been tried out at Brentwood and is dealt with briefly in *Gifted Children and the Brentwood Experiment*.

The first of these stimuli consisted of two incomplete stories with separate forms containing small differences for boys and girls. One story was about the failure of a child to fit into a first-year class in a secondary school and the other about a failure in boxing for the boys and dancing for the girls. The hope was that the children would place themselves emphatically in the situation of the boy or girl about whom they were writing. The situations were feasible but presented problems and it was expected that the children would resolve these problems realistically or else by fantasy. It was assumed that some youngsters would choose what others would consider a far-fetched or fairy-like change, so that the clumsy-footed dancer would overnight become a successful performer, and that others would suggest a solution in the form of a change of activity which might offer greater scope. A third possibility was some credible effort on the part of the failing child to take a grip on himself and so overcome the weakness which had led to his humiliations. As the settings were on the whole serious, expectations were that the completed stories would be mainly serious, although it was hoped that some children would approach the situations in a more light-hearted way. Some examples follow.

One of the girls, believing that practice makes perfect, made her heroine persist in her dancing:

> Emma Jane's mother has always wanted her to be a wonderful dancer and has sent her for dancing lessons. Emma Jane, however, is not very good at dancing; she can hardly keep time to the music. So although she practises more than anyone else and tries her hardest she had not done very well and has never been asked to dance in any of the school shows. She knows that her mother is very disappointed in her. She is disappointed herself because she is really keen on dancing. At last she decides to give it one more try and after she has practised a great deal she is given the chance to do a dance in the show put on by her dancing school. She is too anxious, however, to do well and so

becomes nervous, trips and falls. She feels so upset that she bursts into tears in front of everybody. After the show the dancing teacher tells her that she will never be any good as a dancer. . . . (*Continuation follows.*)

Emma Jane went home very disappointed. She told her mother what had happened. Her mother felt very upset. Emma Jane still went on at her dancing lessons and she tried very hard for a long time. One day two famous people came along because they were going around the country looking for people who will be able to dance at a great concert in London at Christmas time. The girls were told in advance to practise as hard as they could so that they might be chosen for the concert. Emma Jane practised day and night to get her dancing perfect. Then came the great day when the women came. The girls danced for them and at the end they chose Emma Jane to dance in London. She was delighted. She rushed home and told her mother. Her mother said that she would come and watch the concert. At the concert Emma Jane does her dance perfectly and is applauded with honour. It was the beginning of a great career.

One boy felt that the solution lay in trying other sports until Justin found the right one: this young author was himself a very sensible boy and this common sense is the chief characteristic of his story:

Justin's father has always wanted him to be good at sports and to be a member of some of the school teams. Justin is rather a small boy and not very strong: he cannot really run very fast. He has practised very hard but has soon been left out of any team for which he has been chosen. He knows his father is disappointed: he feels disappointed himself since he is very keen on sport. Finally he tries boxing and practises every day. He is picked for a school team and is very pleased. He is so anxious to do well that he makes mistakes and is soon defeated. He is so upset that he bursts into tears before everyone. The sports master sees him and tells him that he will never be any good at sports. . . . (*Continuation follows.*).

Justin just could not help it. When he played rugby he was a total failure because he did not have enough power to run and was certainly not strong enough to push in any scrum. At cricket he had no eye for a ball, and was always out before the first over.

He tried but never seemed to become any better, until one day, about a month after his failure with boxing, he decided to take up fencing. It is not a very tiring sport and not many people, at his school, enjoyed it. He thought that it must be his strong point.

Justin had been learning it for a month now and he was very successful. After two months he decided to enter a competition. He fought his very best and came third out of twenty.

When he grew up, Justin became a professional fencer and won nearly every match he played in.

In the story about a child in a first-year class at a secondary school, one girl felt that the root of the trouble was Elspeth's attitude towards herself, and that when she felt her mother was showing some sympathy she improved, but did not suddenly show signs of genius:

Elspeth is in the first year of secondary school. Things have gone badly for her since the first day. She has not done very well in her work and she knows that one or two of the teachers whom she likes think that she is rather thick. She never seems to think of the right answer when she is asked a question in class. She does not seem to get on very well with the other children. They make a fool of her in class and in the playground. When anything goes wrong teachers and children seem to blame her. One day she hears two girls talking about her: they say that nobody likes her and that she is no use at anything. Elspeth feels that she cannot put up with this any longer. . . . (*Continuation follows.*)

She confides in her mother. Her mother suggests that she tries too hard and must try not to. Elspeth is a friendly girl normally so she must learn to show other people. Her mother also told her to laugh at herself. Elspeth thought this over but then she kept thinking that her mother was not in her position.

However the next day she went to school with this subject fresh on her mind. She was determined to do what she could.

She realized it would not be easy as everybody was set against her. A week later she found it was nice to laugh at herself and she was more relaxed. She was getting a lot more sleep and she found, gradually, she was improving at lessons. At the end of a month all these things had helped gain friendship. At work she could never be very good but you could not call her thick. She gained self-confidence and she never fell in that rut again.

Another girl, who was in the process of maturing and finding herself, made Elspeth run away and then return to school of her own accord. Somehow or other Elspeth as a result made one friend and, as the other girl was very popular, gradually Elspeth acquired friends and her work improved remarkably. In dealing with her failing dancer, this authoress seemed about to introduce humour when she pointed out that Emma Jane's mother, on hearing of her daughter's failure, developed a terrible headache. Then there is a mysterious voice, reminding one of Joan of Arc, which had a tremendous effect on Emma Jane. This story does reveal a certain amount of psychological insight into the needs of Emma Jane:

On hearing this news, her mother develops a terrible headache, and retires to bed. Emma Jane is left alone to ponder upon her unhappy thoughts. At last she cries herself to sleep, and in her dreams she saw a lonely figure of a girl dancing in a huge hall. Suddenly the figure trips and falls. Then she bursts into tears. She remains on the floor, crying until she hears a voice.

"Don't give up. Get up and carry on. Follow the music, relax, and the dancing will come."

When Emma Jane wakes up she is refreshed and feels confident. She then dons her costume and starts practising the dance. She follows the smooth beat of the music and finds herself confident and dancing beautifully. Her mother, at that moment, entered the room and when she saw Emma Jane dancing, she stood watching in amazement.

The next lesson Emma Jane had she followed the music again and the teacher immediately saw a wonderful change.

Emma Jane's new found talent flourished and the next year she was the star of the show, She performed perfectly and was accepted into the Royal School of Ballet.

Finally, it was left to a boy to attempt a more humorous approach in both stories. According to him Justin feels that the sports master has a grudge against him and so is deliberately pitting him against opponents stronger than himself. As his father is clearly upset, Justin decides that on the following morning he will leave the house for school as usual, but instead of going to school he will run away to his uncle:

> "Tomorrow when I go to school I can jump on the bus and go to him." The next day he crams his satchel full of food and other necessaries and goes to the bus stop. Then he can see the bus lumbering towards him. Yes! it is the 72 and it stops before him. Justin hesitates, looking at his Rubicon.
> "Coming lad? Jump on!" exclaims the conductor.
> Justin replies: "I beg your pardon! I'm only waiting for someone."

What stood out here was the boy's sense of climax and anti-climax: a very bright boy, he could see that he had made his point and that there was no need for elaboration or explanation. The same qualities were manifest in his quite brief completion of the story of the unfortunate Oswald. Not only did he evince a sense of humour but he showed also a high degree of empathy, so much so that one tends to wonder whether the story was an autobiographical echo of some personal experience. Perhaps readers will detect, as the present writer seemed to do, a suggestion of Thurber or O. Henry:

> Oswald is in the first year of the secondary school. Things have gone badly for him since the first day. He has not done very well in his work and he knows that one or two of the teachers whom he likes think that he is rather thick. He never seems to think of the right answer when he is asked a question in class. He does not seem to get on very well with the other children. They make a fool of him in the classroom and in the playground. When anything goes wrong teachers and children seem to blame him. One day he hears two boys talking about him: they say that nobody likes him and that he is no use at anything. Oswald feels that he cannot put up with this any longer. . . .
> and so he walks back despondently to his classroom and enters

with the other children as the bell goes. Mr Turwing comes in and announces a Brooke Bond competition for composition. Oswald thought, "O! Smithers will get that. He's the only likely one. What about me? Despised by everyone. . . . " He wrote whatever came into his head, about a boy called Lafindeen whom he put exactly in his position. He hoped that Mr Turwing would read it and might guess that it was himself he was writing about. He studied the teacher's face as he read the essays. A laugh at Roberts, a nod at Smithers and just nothing in his case.

Some time later the results came through together with the teacher's comments:

First, Lasens	Excellent
Second, Smithers	Unpunctuated
Eighth, Oswald	Good. Rather imaginative. Could not be true.

On the whole the children seemed to enjoy this type of stimulus, but they had to be encouraged to write a reasonable amount and so in the next story completion exercise a minimum of 250 words was called for. Only one or two of the pupils failed to reach this number, which was in fact exceeded in several stories. Even here, however, there was evidence of "the stint" approach, especially amongst some of the boys, in the periodic counting and registering of the number of words. With one exception the girls wrote freely and paid little attention to how many words they had written.

In this instance again the children were merely invited to continue a story for at least 250 words, and there was neither injunction nor expressed encouragement to make the stories interesting. It was hoped that the beginning of the story itself would contain sufficient divergent elements to provide an adequate stimulus. It was as follows:

The boy stood in front of the furniture shop looking at his appearance in a mirror in the showcase. He racked his brains trying to remember who he was and where he had come from. There was nothing in the pocket of his short-sleeved shirt or in the pockets of his shorts to help him. The sun-tan on his face, arms and legs suggested that he had spent a lot of time in the sun. Through his mind echoed the words "Seventeen to-day" but it seemed unlikely that he himself was a boy of seventeen. "What shall I do?" he asked himself. . . .

Most of the youngsters brought up on television, radio and comics decided that the best course for the boy was to seek the help of the police. In some other instances the boy willy-nilly found himself in the hands of the police, who usually soon discovered that he was listed as missing. Occasionally the fact that he was sun-tanned suggested an exotic influence, but he still found his way to the police. The words "Seventeen to-day," which were meant to provide an opportunity of heightening the mystery, were sometimes ignored or else they were explained away as a sign of the proximity of the birthday celebrations of a sibling. Indeed, as one should probably expect with a group of children whose logic was pretty highly developed, most of the explanations were largely logical and lacking in mystery, romance or creativity. The general standard of work was higher than that in the previous story-completion, but only a few showed qualities which one was hoping to find.

As an additional exercise and as a further attempt to probe their attitudes to creative and imaginative work, the stories of one group were read to the other group and vice versa. The children were invited to evaluate each story under three headings: Originality, Relevance and Interest. Originality was defined as freshness of approach and unusual ideas; Relevance, as the incorporation of all the detail provided in a meaningful way into the story: obviously, if a pupil completely ignored the words "sun-tanned" or "Seventeen to-day," the mark for Relevance would be materially reduced. Interest required no special definition except that it was in relation to each listener. There were three grades of mark: "a" for an outstanding effort; "b" for good but not so good as "a," and "c" was given to any which did not rate "a" or "b." There were, of course, some wide variations in the evaluation, as is to be expected in subjective scoring: nevertheless there was on occasion a remarkable unanimity, as in the case of 11 c's for one story for Interest. It was noticeable that by far the stiffest assessments occurred under the heading of Relevance. For example one girl received 7 a's and 4 b's for Originality and 5 a's and 6 b's for Interest, but on

Relevance her score was 8 b's and 3 c's. Another girl who had 6 a's and 5 b's for Originality and 5 a's and 6 b's for Interest had 6 b's and 5 c's for Relevance. Indeed, only two boys received a's for Relevance: one whose work is quoted below made a quite ingenious use of the words "Seventeen to-day," while the other boy rounded off his story so well, by concluding with the boy standing outside the furniture shop, that some of the audience did not notice that he had failed to mention these important words.

Of the four which the children judged to be the best, especially in Originality and Interest, two were by girls, one of whom contrived to escape from the usual police situation: instead she treated it as a daydream of temporary aberration in school, but it proved to be a little shorter than was asked for. When this was pointed out to the children, they adhered to their decision, explaining that the story was complete and so extra words were unnecessary.

"What shall I do?" he asked himself, "Where shall I go?" He searched again through his pockets, wondering vaguely what had happened after the explosion. There had been a loud clap of thunder, and something had burst into flames before him. Then he had found himself staring at a boy exactly like himself, very dirty, dishevelled, and, no, it wasn't possible, but if that was a mirror he was looking into, then he had actually been crying! Suddenly, in a flash, it all came back to him. It was his birthday, he was seventeen, his name was Bert Grimsbey, and he had been in the Chemistry lab. when "it" had happened! Vaguely he wondered what had happened to the others, but then he came back to present day facts. Aloud he said:

"How on earth did this mirror get here if there was a fire? *If* there was a fire, and *if* this mirror is real?"

He reached out a hand to touch it, but something warm, hard and hairy touched it before he could go any further. A voice said, harshly but fairly kindly,

"Don't do that, you silly boy! Don't you know that that's *!!?!!***??" He started, and opened his eyes to see a naked gas flame in front of him, and all the other boys laughing at him.

"All right, you! Get back to your work! And as for you, don't do it again!"

The other girl introduced the police into the story but only to link the finding of the boy and the seeking of help from a psychologist, a variation which appealed greatly to the members of the adjudicating panel. There were signs of the authoress having enjoyed herself in the writing of the story but the tell-tale number of words written appeared up to 270: after that, time, and not the number of words, became the decisive factor. It was relatively late in the story before she was able to mention the words "Seventeen to-day," but she succeeded ingeniously towards the end — the word "ingeniously" was actually suggested by one of the audience.

"What shall I do?" he asked himself. The day was getting late and knowing there was no place for him to sleep — because he knew of nowhere, he settled himself on a public bench, and, amidst all worries he fell asleep. At about 10.30 p.m. a hand was laid upon his shoulder — he awoke immediately.

"Nowhere to sleep lad?" He recognized the owner of the voice to be a policeman. The boy shook his head.

"What's your name?" Again the boy had no reply.

"I can't remember my name, where I came from, or anything" he said.

Doing his best to look sympathetic the policeman took him to the local police-station where the boy stayed the night. During the night I had a phone-call. It was from the police-sergeant. I, being a psychologist, was very interested in what he had to tell me. In the morning I gathered some simple test sheets, and bringing him round to my house set them to him. Often he looked puzzled, but I talked, and asked consistently about himself. The data at the end of the week was quite pleasing. Then I gave him a selection of books to read. As if by instinct his hand reached for a book called "The West Indies" then puzzled, he looked at me.

"It meant something to me" he said, "as if I knew it"

I now had a strong suspicion that he had come from the West Indies. By the end of the month I had established that he had some strong link with boats.

To find out more about this I took him to a nearby harbour. Suddenly he shouted, "Look, there!" and pointed to a boat. "We should be on it . . . " then he stopped puzzled once more. I took him aboard. Once on the deck we could see beyond the harbour. A local vendor was shouting out the price of his fruit, "17 to-day!"

The boy suddenly seemed to suffer a great shock, and suddenly it all came back.

"That's what the captain of the ship said, when we left the island." I managed to piece the rest of the story from him and found his anxious parents — emigrants from Jamaica.

The third story, which was highly valued on Originality and Interest, though rather lowly on Relevance, was a strange mixture, and there was some difficulty in determining why the children found it original and interesting. It involved the police and a train crash and finally faded out on a note of fantasy, because time had expired. Certainly one was left wondering whether the story would ever have come to an end in any other way. Although it was basically chronological, there was some evidence of a curious pre-occupation with the passage of time.

"What shall I do?" he asked himself. Then a governor from an orphanage walked up to him and asked if anything was wrong. He said that he did not know where he was or who he was. The governor took him to a police station, where he was asked all sorts of questions. His picture was taken, and put in the papers all over England.

Ten days went by, twenty, thirty, and no reply from his parents.

The governor put him up at the orphanage until someone wrote identifying him. No one wrote for half a year, then, one day, a letter came into the police station. It identified him as Peter Stephens, who had been lost coming back from a year in Australia. He had been lost for a year and a half. His age was fifteen. He was to be picked up at 12.30 p.m. on the Thursday. The day was Friday, so he had six days to wait.

When the Thursday came, he was picked up, and driven to a station. He was taken to Bristol. Then on a small train, he was being taken to a small town, when the train crashed. He was the only survivor. He stumbled about, thinking about how close

he was to living a normal life. Then he decided to go to the
town that he had been going to.

When he got to the town, there was no sign of life, so he
walked around, trying to find some food. He walked round for
half an hour, looking everywhere. Then, suddenly, he heard a
lot of noise. He looked around, and saw about thirty men, run
ning at him. They all held clubs or sticks, and some held dust-
bin lids as shields. They were just about to club him, when

The fourth story was the most ingenious but again it was some
50 words short of the minimum asked for. This story was written
by a boy who tended to express himself in a facetious way whenever possible. Whether he had developed this as a kind of defence
mechanism against older siblings, or whether it was just his nature,
it was difficult to determine. This approach sometimes proved
rather irritating to one or two members of the staff, who regarded
the boy as rather conceited and a nuisance, especially when he tried
to cap remarks made by class-mates, sometimes with a measure of
success. On occasion he made a similar attempt with a remark from
a teacher, and to some adults this seemed impertinent. To others
it appeared to be evidence of a natural mental liveliness, which was
hard to suppress and which was not always unwelcome. Mostly his
written work was extremely brief, although he was less inhibited
on paper than two or three of the other boys. When the brevity
was drawn to the attention of the assessors there was general
agreement that length was of little consequence in his story since
it was complete in itself. When the children were asked whether
they thought the author should be asked to elaborate on his story
the consensus of opinion was that he should not be asked to do
so. Two reasons were advanced: firstly, and perhaps significantly,
that the author would be bored if he were asked to perform the
same exercise again, and secondly, that the story would almost
certainly be spoiled, whereas in its present form it was written
without wasting words. The children seemed to be seeking such
epithets as "economical" and "laconic." When the group were
asked whether they considered the idea of the boy reverting to
twelve years of age, and then growing up again until he was seventeen and repeating the process throughout time, a suitable idea,

on which they themselves might base a story, there was a pause before anyone ventured a reply. One reaction was that it might be suitable after they had reached seventeen, but that was some years off yet. Others seemed to agree with this almost with relief, as if some at least had recognized that basically this was a horror story rather than the amusing and supercilious tale that their fellow pupil had made of it.

"What shall I do?" he asked himself. It was getting dark and he was very worried. His name was Simon. He had just woken up. Or at least that's what it seemed like.

He walked further up the street towards the police station, stopped, turned round, and started back down the street, turned into a side street and sat down. He started to cry. Slowly he slipped down into oblivion.

About five hours later, he awoke. What had happened was that, five years later, on his seventeenth birthday, he was destined to build a time machine. In this he would travel back to his twelfth birthday. This had happened and would keep on happening until he could rebuild the time machine and make it so that he could travel forward in time to one day after his seventeenth birthday or never to die and never to live over seventeen.

That day he brought together all the bits and pieces of the machine and started to build his time-machine. He finished two years later and decided to experiment. The poor fool had forgotten to lubricate it. He travels on to the end of time itself. Goodbye Simon, see you at the end of time.

Perhaps it can be left to the reader to make his own assessment of the quality of the work just quoted, but it is necessary to point to two developments in the experience of the children, arising from these discussions and evaluations. The first of these was that they began to show a greater understanding of what was being sought for when they were given these essays to write. They were beginning to realize that they should try to write interestingly: otherwise no one would be interested enough to read their efforts. But to write interestingly one must oneself feel an interest, and so one must approach a set topic as imaginatively as possible.

Secondly, some at least were now able to perceive that frequently one must put something of oneself into a story; hence it is often easier for a writer to produce an interesting story if it is written in the first person. As a result of further discussions, several of the children began to realize that if an author puts something of himself into a story then the readers of the story may learn something about the author. This finding was not greatly stressed at this point because of the next attempt at creativity.

This attempt consisted of the use of a number of projective pictures which were devised originally for the investigation of children with problems and also for therapeutic use. The pictures themselves are deliberately vague but they show children in many situations in relation to adults and other children. Some are much more provocative and stimulating than others: even so, when they were employed as aids to creative writing many of them produced an orthodox response. In the clinical situation the cards would be given to the boy or girl to evoke a response which would normally be fairly brief, but in the class-room situation each child was given three or four cards, which were carefully chosen according to the helpful classification of the psychologist, whose ideas they were. Each child had at least one card based on the relationships between children and at least one based on that between children and adults. The instructions were to look carefully at each picture which they had been given, and then to write the story suggested by the picture in not less than 50 words: an assignment involving 150 to 200 words seemed reasonable for a period of forty minutes. Needless to say, there were those children who did the bare 50 words each time, while there were others who wrote so much on one card that they had to limit themselves severely on the others. As the cards were used with three different groups of children, several were responded to by at least two children and a few actually by three, but no attempt was made to ensure that the same sets of cards were used in all three groups.

When the stories were read, little attention was paid to style, and the criterion for being worthwhile was that the story should be at least interesting or that it should show some humour. This latter quality was rare, partly because a fair proportion of the pictures are at least potentially grim. An example of the humorous approach is to be found in the work of the boy referred to previously as rather aggressive. The stimulus picture showed what appeared to be two boys, one sitting on one side and the other lying on the other side of a narrow chasm between two cliffs. The pupil's version was:

> "And yesterday I . . . " his voice was broken off. Bang! He landed with a bump. "You all right?" I said. He was. "I'll throw down a rope, and if you grab it, I'll pull you up." That was all right. Fred had reached thirty feet up when Charlie said: "What are you holding on to the rope with?" "My teeth!" said Fred. Bang!

This is the kind of story which has been popular with comedians on the music hall stage and on television for a long time past.

Another of the pictures showed what appeared to be a boy trying to help another boy who had slipped over the edge of a cliff but had somehow managed to arrest his fall. Only one boy in the three groups had this picture and he produced a completely factual story: it is quoted here only because another boy, at an earlier time, had produced a very practical but much more imaginative picture.

The first story read:

> "Help me! Derrick, come quickly," the boy shouted at the top of his voice. "Help! I'm falling." John ran to the side of the cliff just in time to see a boy about five inches shorter than himself slip over the side. The boy landed on a ledge a little way down the cliff. John lay on his front and put his hand over the side of the cliff and got hold of the boy's hand. He pulled him up.

This was, in a sense, the story of the picture, but it contained nothing of the author except perhaps the reference to height. The other story, by a 12-year-old boy of high IQ who was the eldest of a family of four boys, was as follows:

> When I met James to play with him, he was disgruntled because his mother had just washed his jeans and he had had to wear his shorts. Later we were to be glad of this. When we were

at the edge of the cliff, showing off and daring each other, James slipped. Luckily he landed on a little ledge so that I was just able to reach him. With one hand on the stump of a tree, I managed to help him to climb a little so that he was able to put one hand on another little stump and hold on. Then I reached down with my free hand and got my fingers into the legs of his shorts and so I was able to help him to heave himself up. He was rather scared and he had grazed his knees a little, but we were both happy that it had been washing-day.

Not only was the style vastly superior to that of the other, but the boy had worked out the story in detail. Perhaps since he had so many younger brothers his story owed something to personal experience.

One boy, with a fairly high IQ but a moderate creativity rating, tried to be humorous throughout, but he became grim in two of his short stories:

Courageous Silly beckoned to her two friends to follow her. She was going to try and make a parachute and use it herself. Before long she came out of her house with a sheet, tied at the corners, in her hands. She told her companions that she was going to jump out of her bedroom window, three storeys up. God rest her soul.

Jane fell down! John, having just arrived, asked what had happened.
"A car has just run me down," said Jane.
"We had better go to the police," John commented.
"I don't think I can. My leg has gone numb," Jane cried.
"I hope that it is not broken." She got up. Her leg fell off.

Another boy, whose creativity rating had been consistently low, partly because when he was called upon to undertake any written work, other than mathematics, he wrote only one or two sentences, responded fairly orthodoxly but at much greater length than was expected. A year earlier one would have anticipated at

most about twenty words, whereas, in his fourth story, he wrote
as follows:

> Once upon a time a man was taking a boy into a cave. He
> jumped into the river that came out of the cave. It was quite
> warm. The boy jumped in as well, they swam into the cave and
> climbed out of the water. As he was climbing out the boy
> slipped and fell back into the water, yelling very loudly. The
> shout was so loud that it caused an avalanche which blocked
> the mouth of the cave. The water began to rise and they made
> their way along the cave so as not to drown. Quite soon so
> much water had built up behind the blockage that it pushed it
> away. They went back down the cave and got out safely.

The other remarkable feature of this story was that it was
inspired by a picture apparently showing two figures at the side
of a stream approaching a small cave, from which the river flowed.
In other words, the greater part of the story was the result of an
imaginative effort of a kind which the boy, the possessor of a very
high IQ, would not have made even a few months before.

The usefulness of some of these pictures is illustrated by the
following story, inspired by the picture which we have just been
discussing. The authoress is a girl of high ability and with a high
score on creativity.

> How had it happened? The two children looked at each
> other, but neither knew the answer. They were no taller than
> insects and were looking through a mouse-hole near the corner
> of their bedroom wall. Through the hole a red carpet stretched
> and they felt it was meant for them. Walking along it through
> the hole they arrived in a huge market place: within it many
> people of their own height were cheering. They saw that the
> carpet forked in two just beyond the crowd and it was sign-
> posted rather oddly. One "path" led to "William the Conqueror"
> and the other to "Henry VIII." Then they realized that the
> people were saying, "Welcome to those who can go back into
> history." Then a man came up to them and said that they must
> choose a path and follow it to their respective monarchs. Every
> ten years two people had to be selected to change history

very slightly. They were told that it was for making a better world.

Two further illustrations are taken from the work of a boy of thirteen who scored over 150 on the Terman—Merrill and who also scored well on some of the creativity tests, which did not require neat work. Most of the written work which he submitted was adorned with drawings or diagrams or mystic signs. The first sample of his work was inspired by a picture which showed a lady with a long dress and hood apparently offering a violin to a child; the latter was too vague to be identified clearly as a boy or a girl. The story was as follows:

> Once upon a time there was a little bear who wanted to pretend to be a human being. He tried to ape humans in every way: he wore clothes and shoes and he lived in a house but he was still not satisfied. He at last decided that he would like to play a musical instrument and so he chose the violin. However the only place one could buy violins at that time was at a nunnery and so he bought it from one of the nuns.

The other story was based on a picture which to most people would show a small boy or girl standing between two tall men, with one of the men pointing to the child. Our young author wrote:

> Once upon a time were two men and they were passing through their second childhood. They had dolls' houses and they played Mothers and Fathers without the slightest idea of homosexuality. One day they were playing Mums and Dads and they found a Cindy doll. Both of them loved Cindy dolls and they then had a dispute as to whom it should belong.

Whatever the psychologist may divine from a perusal of this story, it should be noted that the boy, at the time of writing, was passing through a stage of finding delight in the use of long words.

Of the more interesting stories the following is a good example. It is taken from the work of the very bright boy, whose work was quoted on pages 102—3. The picture in this instance was a relatively orthodox one, showing two people, probably boys, sitting fishing.

One of the boys has just been successful in catching a fish. This inspired the boy to write:

Sir John Spark, "Bright" to all his friends, had had, since early childhood, a passion for inventing. Many times his career had been likened to that of the infamous Dr Braainstorm. His latest invention had been a revolutionary kind of fish-bait. When the bait was put in the water it turned all the water near-by mustardy. As the fish, affected by the mustardy water, naturally wishes for something cool it makes its way towards a piece of ice which forms the main part of the bait. The fish swallows it and it is so cold that it freezes the mouth of the fish so that it clamps around the hook and can be pulled up. For the first time it was to be experimented with and he took a schoolboy along with him. What happened was not quite what he had expected. The mustard made the fish so hungry that they made for the boy's conventional bait and so he landed a bumper catch. "Ah!" explained Sir John, never to be beaten, "All it needs is some one to bait the fish into a temper so that he eats the ice by mistake."

9
Self-understanding

As already pointed out, the present studies were less concerned
with intellectual development than some of the earlier ones in the
field of Gifted Children, partly because of the need to assume that
the children were being adequately challenged in their subjects
and partly because so many of them were uncertain of themselves.
Not only did a fair number of them tend to undervalue themselves
and their abilities, but a number of them also showed little understanding of themselves. The majority had accepted the conditioning
which had been exerted on them by adult society, including their
schools, and it was in fact this acceptance that led to so many of
them persistently under-achieving. Others were at least superficially
less satisfied but only a few of them were able to analyse situations
in which they found themselves. Some of the creative projective
techniques and the discussions had helped in some cases, but it
seemed both advisable and necessary to make use of more direct
methods, though it was not clear what these methods should be.

The obvious answer seemed to be to use some personality tests
and inventories, but when these were used certain difficulties
arose, some from the test themselves and others from the children's
reactions to them. As far as possible the term "test" was avoided
and in the instructions it was explained that in these "inventories"
or "exercises" there was no question of a right or wrong answer.
Unfortunately, some of the printed personality inquiries are officially called "tests" as, for example, the 16PF Test, and wherever
the word "test" occurred some children reacted in the way they
had been conditioned to do throughout their school lives. However,
as the children became more familiar with his particular technique

they began to ignore the term"test" but then they raised other objections.

A second difficulty was that most of the "tests" readily available were intended for adults and near-adults. One very useful British Personality Inventory for children had already been applied to one or two of the children at a clinic, and so was ruled out. At the same time, as it was felt that most of these children had the reasoning powers of adults, there was an argument for using adult inventories despite certain obvious difficulties. One of these was the assumption that the person being studied was in employment of some kind. When the children had to fill in their occupation most of them ignored the invitation, but others put "schoolboy" or "schoolgirl" or "student." Two or three boys preferred to state that they were "unemployed," which was perhaps nearer the truth than they thought. In certain cases they had to be told that they must assume they were adults in employment and make their choice of answers accordingly.

A third difficulty lay in the fact that most of the tests available were American and these had to be used, but some of the items were rather unsuitable for British conditions. It was not just a matter of the different school usages: for example, the common use of "school" where British people would refer to college, or even the use of the term "kids" for boys and girls up to the age of 21 or so, as is so common in the United States. There were also references to such activities as "family conferences," which the British children regarded as amusing or even ridiculous. Sometimes interpretation proved necessary.

A fourth difficulty arising from the "tests" themselves was the length of the usual American "test" or inventory. Most had over a hundred items and the time available each week was such that there was always a certain amount of pressure required to ensure that the slower workers or the more deliberate children would finish the questions in one session.

A fifth difficulty lay in the availability of suitable norms. Fortunately, the NFER has gathered some British norms for some of the American tests so that preference was given to these. On the other hand, norms for children of the age of our experimental groups were rarely available, since these tests were not as a rule used with children below their late teens. It is, of course, doubtful whether norms mean very much in the personality "tests": the children were more interested in comparing each other's profiles, where the tests used made this possible.

Three difficulties arose from the children themselves. One of these was an unwillingness to approach the exercises imaginatively when called upon to do so. Sometimes they were confronted with an adult problem, for example, that of making a decision as a parent; some of the children seemed to appreciate the challenge implied in having to make an adult decision, but others would say that as school-children they could not make such a decision. Others again would protest that the situation, of American origin, had no connection with their own lives in Britain, and even when the British equivalent was outlined to them a few were still reluctant to express a view. This kind of difficulty never quite disappeared: even in the penultimate meeting with one group at Millfield, when a Leadership test was tried out, there were some who still voiced their protest.

The second of the children's difficulties lay in an unwillingness on the part of some to give themselves away by their answers. This unwillingness, amounting to resentment at times, had been shown in the earlier meetings when the children had first been called on to respond to certain projective exercises. With the increased trust that had grown up in the groups as they became more certain of the confidentiality observed towards their work, most of the unwillingness disappeared, but from time to time there was a recrudescence in some boys and girls.

The final difficulty lay in the recurring resentment against some of the forced-choice items. Children frequently protested against having to make a choice, despite the fact that the directions for all the inventories pointed out that it could occur that the children might find it hard to make a decision. The instructions usually said that where this situation arose the children should compel themselves to make a choice. In other cases the children maintained that they did not like either alternative and so it was really impossible for them to make a sensible choice. In discussion on this difficulty, one boy, who had protested on several occasions and who, despite frequent cajoling, had once or twice failed to enter an answer, expressed his opinion thus: "It is like my sister asking me whether I would prefer to wear one of her skirts or one one of her frocks, whereas in fact I have no wish to wear either." This view was given much support in the group, which felt that it was a perfect analogy and quite unanswerable. It was noticeable, however, that after this discussion the group showed less resentment, but whether it was a case of *post hoc ergo propter hoc* it would be hard to prove.

One problem which arose in connection with all the personality exercises was whether the results of the "tests" should be given to the children either individually or as a group. When the views of the pupils were sought, the majority declared at once that they had no objection to the other boys and girls knowing how they had fared. One or two children were hesitant but their curiosity seemed to overcome their scruples and in most of the groups there was ultimate unanimity. The author was uncertain, in particular, about revealing the results of sociometric tests of desired group companions, and consequently he did not make use of negative preferences, but when he tried to maintain confidentiality by using a sociogram with letters instead of names, some astute members of the group had cracked the code within a few minutes. This group then demanded an explanation of sociograms, which they seemed to find interesting, even when they were shown on a particular criterion to be isolates or near-isolates. It was because of this interest and this demand that the sociograms chosen were the ones pertaining to that group.

The group consisted of 8 boys and 4 girls, most of the children having IQ scores of 140 or over on either the Terman—Merrill or the WISC. They were told that it was hoped to divide the group into sub-groups of 4 children each, and they were invited to write down the names of the 3 children with whom they would like to work. No mention was made to the pupils about whether the sub-groups should contain both boys and girls, and as the children were about 12 years of age there was no great surprise when the results showed that boys had chosen boys and that the girls had decided they would make a very good group together. Each of the girls then had three choices, all mutual. The boys' results were more varied.

Sociogram No. 1

Choices received

		B1	B2	B3	B4	B5	B6	B7	B8
	B1		X		X		/		
	B2	X				X		/	
Choices made	B3	/	/				/		
	B4	X		/				X	
	B5	/	X	/					
	B6		/			/		/	
	B7	/		/	X				
	B8		/		/	/			
Total choices		5	5	3	3	3	2	3	0

Mutual choices are crossed

Both B1 and B2 were really clever boys and it was natural for the others to choose them on a criterion of working together, but they differed in their approach from other people, including other pupils. B1 was a genial boy who easily established good relationships with others, whether older or younger. B2, on the other hand was rather conscious of his superior ability and did not suffer fools gladly. The most surprising feature of the sociogram was that he had been chosen in preference to B1 by B8, the youngest boy in the group, who tended to be also the shyest. Later in discussion B8 revealed that his choice had been dictated by two facts. One was that B2 was bright and would make a good leader but the other was that he realized B1 was popular and would have a lot of choices, so that he was unlikely to find a place in his group: he did not expect B2 to be overwhelmed with choices. Shy this boy was, but he showed here a perception which was ultimately to help him largely to overcome his shyness. When he learned that nobody had chosen him he was not surprised because he knew he was not making much impression on the other children in the group. As he was a day-boy, he lacked the opportunities that the boarders had for making friends, but he had still some friends at home in the village, where he had been at school. B2 reminded the group that as a boarder, such as he was himself, he could have made enemies as well as friends: some of the other boarders agreed with this statement.

There was one rather surprising feature of the sociogram, and that was the failure of some boys to choose each other. B5, B6 and B7 formed a little group who came from the same class and who were frequently in each other's company: two of them were in the same house. It was expected that they would show some mutual choices amongst themselves, but the sociogram shows that they did not choose according to expectation. B6 chose B5 and B7. He was the most dependent of the three boys; but while B5 and B7 both took B1 as their first choice, they did not choose one another. The explanation was that they paid strict attention to the criterion of working together. If they had been all together in a group, they felt that not a great deal of work would have been done. Instead, B5 opted for B2, who was bright and who had some authority over him: hence, perhaps, the mutual choice; while B7 opted for B4, who was bright and who had been in the same boarding-house with him for over two years.

As soon as it became clear that the boys had chosen boys only, and the girls, girls only, it was suggested to the children that it would be better to have three mixed groups, and so they were invited to choose again, each boy making certain that he included at least one girl in his group, and each girl including at least one boy in her choices. After one or two of them had demurred a little, the youngsters began making their new choices. with the results shown in Sociogram No. 2. While the children were making their choices, one of the boys asked whether he was limited to choosing one girl only. He was told that this was not so and that any pupil might nominate three members of the opposite sex. As the sociogram shows, no boy or girl went as far as this, but in fact B3, B6 and B8 each opted for two girls, whilst two of the girls

Sociogram No. 2

Choices received

		B1	B2	B3	B4	B5	B6	B7	B8	G1	G2	G3	G4
Choices made	B1		X		X					X			
	B2	X				X					X		
	B3	/								/			X
	B4	X						X		/			
	B5		X	/							/		
	B6		/									/	X
	B7	/			X					/			
	B8		/							/		X	
	G1	X									X	X	
	G2		X							X			X
	G3	/						X		/			
	G4			X			X			/			
Total		6	5	2	2	1	1	1	1	7	4	3	3
Mutual Choices		3	3	1	2	1	1	1	1	2	2	2	3

opted for two boys. One of the girls so choosing was G3, who was chosen by two of the boys preferring two girls in their group.

Comparison of the two sociograms revealed several other points of interest. Firstly, the two most popular boys had held their leading positions: they discarded their third-choice boys in favour of one of the more popular girls. The discarded boys had not reciprocated the leaders' choices, whereas the two girls chosen did reciprocate those choices. Secondly, G1 was the most popular choice of all, with five choices from boys and two from girls. G1 was a very bright girl who was also gifted in the social field and was well liked by most people, young or old. It was, perhaps, a little surprising that she had only two mutual choices, whereas both B1 and B2 had the maximum, three. There was, indeed, a remarkable number of mutual choices between boys and girls, five of the seven pairs being in this category. Indications were that this was largely the result of individual likings or sympathies arising from rather different causes in each case.

One feature was that in the group there was no complete isolate, but in the second sociogram there were no fewer than four boys who had only one choice, whereas in the first the corresponding figures had been 3, 2, 3 and 0 choices. It must be mentioned once again, however, that these relationships were in a specialized group and that some of these boys would have scored more highly if the sociometric technique had been applied to their more regular groupings.

Some cases seem to deserve separate mention since we are more interested in the children learning about themselves than about the temporary relationships in a group on one criterion. The first of these is that of B8, who had no choices on the first sociogram but one mutual choice with a girl on the second. B8 has already been described as very young and very shy, and so it was perhaps not surprising that when he was obliged to choose a girl he should opt for G3 who, although intelligent and an obedient scholar, was also rather motherly in character. Her choices included the most popular girl and two boys, B1 as well as B8. They were based on her maternal approach (she was the eldest of a family) rather than on intellectual capability: she admitted that she liked looking after "small" boys.

The second case is that of B2 and G2. The latter was nominated by two boys and two girls, one of the boys being B2 who in turn chose G2 as the one girl with whom he would like to work. B2, as already indicated, was rather bright but rather arrogant in his relationships with other children, and G2 was not unlike him in her attitude to those who were less clever than herself. It had been expected that these two would repel each other or at least ignore each other, but instead they formed a mutual choice. For once it looked like "birds of a feather." This description would not apply to the choices of B6, who, having found that B5 and B7 failed to reciprocate his choice of them, adhered to his first choice of B2 (unreciprocated) and substituted two girls, G3 and G4. These two girls tended to be rather quiet but they were both diligent scholars and both quite mature for their age. The action of the boy was not surprising, but it did seem remarkable that G4 should have reciprocated the choice, as B6 was inclined to be dependent and was certainly less developed socially than the girl. Apart from the fact that B6 and G4 saw a good deal of each other since they were in the same class for most subjects, they had in common a quiet but very pleasant sense of humour and it may have been this that brought them together.

When the children had heard the results and recovered from the inevitable remarks about the boys and girls who had shown a marked preference for the opposite sex, the sociograms were displayed on an overhead projector. A brief account of the work of J. L. Moreno was given and then questions and comments were invited. As stress had been laid on the great importance of the criterion in effecting the choice, some questions arose about the criterion, as, for example, why work had been selected. It was explained that this had been done because it was meant to fit in with their course, and there was evidence that when people liked each other, and got on well together, the work done tended to be more efficient and less wasteful than when people working together did not like each other or were incompatible in some other way. The children were asked to reflect for a minute or two on what difference it would have made if the criterion chosen had been games. The boys were quick to point out that they would certainly not have chosen girls if the games had been soccer, rugby or cricket. One or two said also that they would have made changes in their choice of boys: some in the group were not good or enthusiastic games-players. The girls thought that they would have made different choices with other criteria but were less emphatic about this than the boys.

One girl asked whether the same result would be arrived at, if choices were asked for, a few months later. She was asked, in turn, whether she herself would repeat her present choices. Several of the children showed eagerness to answer this question and some time was given to the answers, as obviously these would help them to some degree of self-understanding. The consensus of views was that changes would occur for a variety of reasons. One of these was that some children change in their attitudes to each other either because of a disagreement or a quarrel or because some new friend happens along. Another explanation was that the longer you are acquainted with a person the better you come to know him or her. In some cases this greater knowledge might strengthen the friendship but in others the friendship might lessen and ultimately disappear. On being asked if they thought that it was the other person who caused the rift by changing, they agreed that this might be so, but admitted that they themselves might be the ones to change. Several of the children manifested considerable perception in regard to the inevitable changes in relationships and one boy, B1, gave an example in his own experience. He had been very friendly with two boys of his own age at his previous Junior school and when he returned home for the first time, from Edgarley, he had sought them out. They were still very friendly and they welcomed him, but he detected some sort of change. In subsequent holidays he saw less and less of the two boys, who still played together. They had clearly not changed very much and seemed happy together, but a change had occurred and he realized now that it must be in himself. One of the girls admitted that since she had been away from home for two or three years at school, she had found that her relationships with her two brothers, who were younger than she was, had changed. Now, the age gap between herself and them seemed to be growing greater each time she went home on holiday. Another girl had noted that her brother, who used to welcome her home, was now more interested in other girls, and she thought that although, now, boys seemed rather juvenile, she would probably change her views. If she could fill in the list of choices two or three years later, she might choose three boys instead of one.

One boy, B2, wished to know how the sub-groups would be formed (unfortunately, because of certain adverse circumstances, the sub-groups were never formed), since some children were chosen by several others and some had very few choices. It was

explained to the children that such sociograms were indications
of certain preferences but they rarely made it possible to form
groupings without some manipulations. For example, although
B1 and B2 had made a reciprocal choice, so many other children
had chosen them that it would not be possible to have them in the
same group. The obvious procedure was to base the sub-groups
on B1, B2 and G1. Children with only one choice would, if that
were reciprocated, go with their mutual choice. Clearly, there
were several possible groupings, of which one might be: (1) B2,
B5, G2, G4; (2) B1, B4, G3, B8; (3) G1, B7, B3, B6. In this arrangement G1 would be denied any of her reciprocal choices, often one
of the prices paid for being the most popular and being chosen as
a leader, and B6 would have none of his choices in the third sub-
group. Whatever arrangement was made, there would quite often
be one or two children who were unlucky.

The final question was whether the groups formed in this way
were always successful. The honest answer had to be that it was
not necessarily so, as the sociogram showed only a number of
preferences and did not reveal the bases of these preferences.
Unless people were thoroughly familiar with the companions they
chose, the latter might have certain characteristics which would
become noticeable only in the course of a period of working together. For example, a boy who was unsystematic or untidy in his
work might be linked with someone who was very orderly, and
the irritation caused might well destroy the bases for the original
choices. This led to a brief study of toleration, which was recognized as a very important quality. One or two of the children
agreed that they became impatient with other children with whom
they had to work in their ordinary classes. Others then tried to
switch the discussion from incompatibilities between pupils to
incompatibilities between pupils and teachers. They were reminded
that for professional reasons this was a difficult topic to discuss,
but this did not prevent one or two instances being quoted. The
children were urged to examine themselves in any case of incompatibility: it might be on the teacher's side or it might be on the
pupil's side, or it might be that they had mutual incompatibilities.
Some seemed to be unconvinced, but others agreed that they
were often at fault, and so the discussion closed.

Another exercise in self-understanding was inspired by the Myers—Brigg Type Indicator, which is based on certain Jungian categories. The Indicator is hardly meant for children of the age in our groups and was unsuitable itself because it was too long. The children of 10 to 12 were unwilling to face up to answering over 160 items and in any case the lesson periods were too short to permit of the use of some of the longer but more interesting "tests." The Myers—Brigg Type Indicator does, however, explore a number of areas into which we felt the children should enter, and so we chose some of the areas and presented items of the forced-choice type used in the Indicator. Curiously enough, the children did not resent these forced-choice items as they had done and were to do in other instances: indeed this type of approach was well liked, and when the children were invited, later, to suggest which exercise should be repeated in future groups, this one had unanimous support. Perhaps on some occasion it will prove possible to try out the Indicator on the children and so to use the norms which are provided. As this was their first attempt at this kind of work, the children were told two or three times that in giving their preferences there were no right and no wrong answers.

The areas we decided to explore were those of the reactions and feelings of the children in company; their preferences for ideas or facts, imagination or common sense; their beliefs about the relative interests of a child's life and an adult's life; the presence or absence of worries. When their answer sheets had been scored they were given the results for each preference on each item and were invited to compare their own results with those of the group as a whole. They were also allowed to compare their choices with those of other children if they so wished, but the emphasis was to be on their own results rather than on those of the group as a whole or of other children.

The results were very varied but there were one or two that caused some surprise and these were used as the bases of a discussion. For example, in a group of 22 children no fewer than 15 asserted that children have more interesting lives than adults. The 7 who preferred adult life were asked to give their views first. These children chiefly stressed the negative side — adults were free from the tiresome restrictions which parents and teachers inflicted on the young. One or two thought that the adult's life was the more interesting because of the possibilities of marriage and parenthood; others argued that adults had fascinating jobs which were of absorbing interest in contrast to school-work. There was little indication that any of these children realized how many adults have jobs which afford them little pleasure or satisfaction. Several thought that adults were better off because they controlled their money or were able to go to other countries when they felt like it or business required it. The views expressed were, on the whole, those to be expected in any discussion by school-children of average ability.

When the 15 children who had preferred the life of a child were asked for their reasons, ideas flowed freely. The commonest was that adults are in a sense more restricted than children, that they are constantly confronted by problems of running a home, or finding the money for their needs and for their children, and that they have much less time to relax or play than children. Even in a boarding-school there was time set apart each day for play, but this did not apply to adults or teachers who were on duty while children played. Other adult difficulties manifested themselves in the course of the discussion, such as the danger of the break-up of a marriage or illness or overwork, whereas children were free of these, although they might be affected as a result of such misfortunes. Perhaps the most valuable contribution to the discussion was the admission by some boys and girls that they had never seriously considered the matter before, but that since they had had to express a preference they had been thinking about it. They agreed that much might be said on both sides, but after more careful consideration they still adhered to their original view. One boy, extremely bright, remembered that he had accepted the choice as a fair one, but now that he had thought about it he was not so sure that it was. Children's lives could be interesting some of the time and boring at other times; he surmised that this was equally true of adults. He had noted this in his own life, which he enjoyed most of the time, and it seemed to be true also of his parents. When asked whether he thought teachers generally enjoyed their lives he was rather wary, but eventually expressed the view that some certainly did while others seemed rather miserable and unhappy. Other children agreed and volunteered to offer names for the two categories so that the discussion was hastily terminated.

When choosing between imagination and common sense, 9 children favoured the former and 13 the latter, and in another item 15 preferred to be described as persons of common sense as against 7 who preferred to be known as people of imagination. Half of the group preferred to be regarded as practical persons and half as inventive. In the discussion that followed it became clear that some of the children had acquired a stereotyped view about imaginative people as being rather short of common sense and as being frequently unpractical. The children who held this view tried to illustrate it from some of the great artists, literary figures and musicians, but had to agree that there were many such people who had also possessed common sense. Some of the children said that they were often told by their parents, and sometimes by their teachers, that they must learn some common sense. This led to a discussion on what was meant by common sense and a definition proved difficult. A definition of imagination seemed to be easier but some of the definitions would have fitted fantasy rather than imagination. The most valuable outcome of this discussion was that most of the children realized that they had been using both terms, throughout a considerable part of their lives, without having thought about their real meaning. It seemed to them that common sense was desirable but perhaps not very common, while imagination also seemed to be a worthy quality. They appeared to understand that both qualities had their part to play, with common sense restraining imagination in some circumstances and imagination, including inventiveness, outrunning common sense so that progress became possible.

In this particular group, 13 children claimed that they had very few worries while 9 claimed to have a lot of worries. They had, already, on the whole, declared that they were reasonably happy in their school and not too worried about examinations, which were in any case still two or three years ahead, and so it was assumed that the worries must derive mostly from home or from other individual causes. If this was so, 9 seemed a rather high proportion. A long discussion was held but it did not seem to be throwing up anything of value and so it was decided to talk over the matter individually with some of the worried ones. It became obvious that there were one or two genuine worries about the parents: girls were anxious because their father or mother or both were working too hard and so risking a breakdown, and a few children were concerned about disagreements between their parents. Where there we're real causes for worry they came from outside the child, and little could be done to help. One happy-go-lucky boy who claimed to have a lot of worries seemed to present a contradiction between his customary behaviour and attitudes on the one hand and his statement on the other. When he was asked if he had any big worry which was affecting him or his work, he could not think of any but said that on the day he sat the "test" he had been worried that rain would prevent games that afternoon.

A third technique used was an exercise in sentence-completion with the following instructions:

> If you do this exercise carefully you will be helping your teachers to help you. In each case you are given the first part of a sentence — your job is to complete the sentence in any way you like. Write clearly but do not pay too much attention to the spelling, etc. Work as quickly as you can.
> Here is an example: On my birthday . . .
> You might add, "I receive presents" or "I am always happy."

The instructions were deliberately set in a low key: there was no invitation to be imaginative or fanciful, as it was felt that sentences so inspired would not help the children when they came to study their fifty completions and compare them with the corresponding sentences of the other children.

Some examples will reveal the nature of the responses, which were for the most part rather mundane or defensive: the latter, of course, had their value. The fifty part-sentences covered parents, siblings, the child's own desires and ambitions, teachers, homes, the child's feelings, etc. The following examples are taken from the answers of a boy of 12 who scored a maximum on the WISC.

1 When I have nothing to do . . . I always meditate
4 Most parents . . . should be fairly strict on children.

7 I admire a person . . . who plays good football.

13 After school . . . I will go to college.

14 I feel there is nothing worse than . . . living for 200 years.

17 Compared with other children, I feel myself . . . completely independent.

20 Older brothers and sisters . . . are real BULLIES.

26 When people talk of clever children I . . . think of people with complexes.

28 I believe most grown-ups think of me as being . . . unbearable.

33 I am annoyed by people who . . . crack stupid jokes.

41 I often think of myself as a . . . big show-off.

48 Like most people I feel that my family is . . . intelligent.

One report on this boy when he was just over 10 years of age included the remark: "This boy does very well but scarcely lives up to his potential in his present setting. Perhaps the work is not sufficiently demanding but he scarcely gives himself to it in the way I would like to see and constantly ducks a variety of subjects, which may vary from one term to another." Perhaps this links up with his answer to No. 38, which read "The thing that makes me study hardest is . . . " and the boy's answer was "A harsh tutor." Throughout his completions he tended to be too hard on himself, but he was quite obviously maturing rapidly, and the study of himself seemed to be helping. He was still, at 12, both conforming and aggressive, but his aggressiveness arose from a number of causes; he seemed to the author to be one of the most likable and worthwhile children in his group.

A few of the completions provided by children to two of the stimulus phrases may serve to illustrate the variety of responses and so the variety of attitudes.

A boy: 12 Above all, I wish my father were . . . at home more often.

        18 My mother . . . is kind.

A girl: 12 Above all, I wish my father were . . . with me all the time.

        18 My mother . . . is wonderful.

A girl: 12   Above all, I wish my father were . . . happier.
           18   My mother . . . is very helpful when I have a
                 problem.

Several of the children showed anxiety about one or other or both
of their parents, one or two wishing that their parents were younger
and others wishing that the father or mother did not have to work
so hard.

Finally, a sample of answers to two stimuli directly concerned
with the children will give some insight into how some of them
regarded themselves.

A boy, IQ *c*. 140 Terman—Merrill:
           34   I feel my family thinks I am . . . brainy.
           44   I think most people think of me as . . . brainy.
A boy: 34   I feel my family thinks I am . . . a football
                 fanatic.
           44   I think most people think of me as . . . a foot-
                 ball fanatic.
A girl: 34   I feel my family thinks I am . . . a nice girl.
           44   I feel most people think of me as . . . a nice
                 person.
A girl, IQ 152 WISC:
           34   I feel my family thinks I am . . . lucky to come
                 here (Edgarley).
           44   I think most people think of me as . . . childish.
A girl, IQ 156 Terman—Merrill:
           34   I feel my family thinks I am . . . fairly agreeable.
           44   I think most people think of me as . . . unpleas-
                 ant to be with.
A boy, IQ 154 WISC:
           34   I feel my family thinks I am . . . a normal boy.
           44   I think most people think of me as . . . both
                 bearable and unbearable.

In the discussion, which followed the opportunity given to the
children to study what they had written, they asked about certain
letters which had been pencilled in against some of the sentences.
These were merely such letters as "S," to mark where the child

seemed to have revealed something of a personal assessment which had some meaning to an outsider; "F" to pinpoint attitudes on the family, and "A" which marked apparently contradictory statements which seemed to indicate ambivalence. An explanation was attempted of "ambivalence," with uncertain success. There were also brief notes on the top of the front page of each exercise which represented an attempt to summarize the chief trends in the completed sentences. Most of these were to the effect that a favourable attitude to parents had been shown (but one boy who clearly respected his father expressed the wish that his father might become more brainy) and also to grandparents, who mostly were highly esteemed for their generosity and affection. Some of the children were self-critical but the majority were comparatively complacent. The younger children provided some evidence of difficulties with older brothers and sisters and in the discussion two or three boys and girls gave instances of what they were referring to in their sentences. One boy went so far as to assert that he was happier at school when he was away from his brothers. When the children who complained about their siblings were asked whether they themselves might contribute to family disagreements, they admitted that they were perhaps not entirely free from blame. Most of them, on looking over some of the marked items for the last time, before the end of the discussion, felt that the exercise had been useful in making them think about themselves: all the groups who sat this exercise thought that it should be repeated with future groups.

One of the most popular exercises undertaken by the children was Richardson's British version of the Study of Values, adapted from the third edition of the American study devised by Allport, Vernon and Lindzey. There were various reasons for this popularity. One was that the test was adapted to British conditions; another was that each child could draw his own profile, and a third was that the youngsters always seemed to prefer printed tests to those which we had devised and duplicated ourselves.

The Study consists of two parts, in the first of which there are statements or questions which are described as controversial: each statement contains two choices . The candidate has three marks, which he can give to one of the statements if he agrees with it strongly and the other will be marked zero. If he prefers one to the other, but not strongly, he can allocate 2 and 1 marks respectively. In the second part, each statement has four parts and the candidate is asked to list them in the order of his preferences, the first choice receiving three marks, the second two, the third one, and the fourth zero. When the statements have been scored, they are tabulated under six headings: Theoretical, Economic, Social, Aesthetic, Political and Religious. An average male profile and an average female profile are provided; in addition there are tables of ranges for each heading, showing the highest 10 per cent, the next 20 per cent and so on. When the forms were returned to the children after scoring, they were able to draw their own profiles and they found a good deal of interest in comparing their profiles with the average ones given and with those of other children. It had to be explained to them that these were not absolute scores but relative. The table of percentage distribution provided by the publishers was shown to help in establishing how one stood in relation to the original test population.

A sample of the results obtained is given for a group of 20 children, aged 11 to 12+ and with IQs ranging from 2 to 3 Standard Deviations above the mean on the Terman–Merrill and the WISC. Under the heading, "Theoretical," the range was from 28 to 44 for the fifteen boys and from 29 to 45 for the girls. It had been assumed that the mean for this item would have been well above that of the average male and female supplied with the test, but the mean for our bright boys was only 35·4, not much above that of the average male, and the female mean of 35·2 was also only a little above that of the average provided.

Under "Economic" the boys' range was from 21 to 42 with a mean of 33, as against an average of 30 for the test population; the girls' range was from 19 to 31 with a mean of 26·6, which was very slightly below the average provided. Under "Aesthetic" the boys' range was from 12 to 29 with a mean of 22·7, almost exactly that of the average, while the girls' range was from 24 to 37 with a mean of 30·6, about a point above the average given. Under "Social" the boys' range was from 31 to 48 with a mean of 41, this being 2 to 3 points above that supplied, while the girls' range was from 36 to 45 with a mean of 39·6, a little above the test average. Under "Political" the range for the boys was from 11 to 34 with a mean of 25·4, a little below the average, while the girls' range was from 16 to 26 with a mean of 19·2, about two points below the average. Under "Religion," the range of the boys was from 5 to 44 with a mean of 24·8, a little below the average; the girls' range was from 7 to 47 with a mean of 24·8 which was considerably lower than the average. Without two very high scores for the boys, 41 and 44, and two very low ones, 7 and 5, the boys' mean would have been quite near the average; without the 7 and the 47 the girls' mean would have been 30, much nearer the average.

The relatively low mean for the girls in "Religion" came as a surprise, as it was assumed that girls would show up more under this heading, but of course the number of girls involved was very small. What the results as a whole did show up clearly was how varied the views of twenty children of high ability can be, so that any provision which has to be made for them in the educational field must cover a wide range of interests. Although the mean for the girls under "Aesthetic" was very considerably above that of the boys, the range of the latter was 19 as compared with 12 for the girls. Again, in the case of "Political" there was a not unexpected difference between the mean for the boys and that for the girls, but the range of 23 for the boys showed that even such a difference between boys and girls was no firm guide to the nature of the provision required. But these are the lessons for teachers, and the first purpose of the test was to help the children to understand themselves. Some were pleased with the indication that their interests lay in certain favoured areas; others were somewhat surprised. The children who received very low scores in Religious Interests seemed to be highly amused and one boy suggested that his score be reported to the Headmaster and to the teacher in charge of Religious Studies so that he might be exempted from the subject forthwith.

The next attempt at helping in self-understanding was made by using the 16PF Test of Personality which was obtainable from the NFER Publishing Company. But this test is of American origin.

It is called the 16PF as it is intended to cover sixteen personality factors and requires the testee to answer over a hundred items. These items each have three possible answers and are of the type:

I like to play games   (*a*) Yes; (*b*) Sometimes; (*c*) No.

On the back of the answer sheet is a profile on which the tabulated results for the sixteen factors can be shown in stens, with the meanings of the low and high scores respectively being explained.

The first step on this occasion was to give the children the explanations and instructions necessary and then to ask them to sit the test. They were taken aback when they saw the length of it, but as soon as they found that they could answer quickly they began to enjoy it. The answers were then scored and the individual profiles drawn. In the next session the children were given their profiles and invited to study the low and high score descriptions. Once they were sure that they understood the different categories, they were asked to mark with a tick those with which they agreed and with a cross those which seemed seriously wrong. Meanwhile, a sheet with simplified forms of the categories was circulated to the teachers of the children under test, with the rubric:

In the following pairs of words or phrases, underline that which seems the more applicable to the above pupil. If both seem to apply, please ring both words.

When the sheets from the tutors had been returned, the children were given the results for all the tutors, but not, of course, what individual tutors had said. In some cases, as, for example, when every tutor agreed on a factor, the children were soon aware of the individual estimates.

To give some idea of how this worked out the scores for one girl (IQ 152 WISC) were as follows: The profile showed her to be reserved, intelligent, fairly easily upset, half way between humble and assertive, somewhat gay, more inclined to conscientiousness than to expediency, somewhat tender-minded, suspicious, and imaginative, inclined to shrewdness and to apprehensiveness, above average on being liberal, self-sufficient, somewhat affected by undisciplined self-conflict, and very highly tense. The girl agreed with two of the results, disagreed with four and tended to accept the rest as probably right or at least not far wrong. The following list shows her results as well as those of her tutors. Low sten scores favour the factor on the left, high that on the right.

Sten Score	Self	Tutors		Tutors		Sten Score
3	✓	Reserved	3	Warm-hearted	3	—
—	—	Concrete thinking	2	Abstract Thinking	5	8
4	✓	Affected by Feelings	4	Emotionally Stable	3	—
5	—	Obedient	4	Assertive	2	—
—	X	Serious	6	Enthusiastic	2	7
—	—	Disregards Rules	0	Conscientious	6	6
5	—	Shy	5	Adventurous	1	—
—	—	Tough-minded	3	Tender-minded	3	6
—	✓	Practical	3	Imaginative	3	6
—	X	Forthright	3	Shrewd	3	7
—	—	Self-assured	2	Apprehensive	5	9
—	X	Conservative	4	Experimenting	3	7
—	—	Socially Group-dependent	0	Self-sufficient	6	6
4	X	Uncontrolled	2	Controlled	4	—
—	X	Relaxed	3	Tense	4	10
—	—	Trusting	4	Suspicious	3	6

In certain respects this girl who was very withdrawn and at times almost taciturn appeared to impress all her teachers in much the same way, whereas in others there was a large measure of disagreement or uncertainty. Although the girl disagreed at times both with the test and with the verdicts of some of her teachers, she admitted that when she was preoccupied with her problems, some of which were concerned with home, it must be difficult for teachers to understand her. On the other hand she was sometimes bored in certain subjects and so would not appeal to the teachers concerned.

In the discussion which followed on the use of the 16PF and also the High School Personality Questionnaire, a junior form of the 16PF, there was a consensus in favour of tests of this type, although some children felt that the categories were sometimes hard to understand. They enjoyed the tests, and some were fascinated by the profiles, with which on the whole they expressed agreement, although where disagreement did occur it could be very

strong. Generally, there was amusement at the verdicts of the
tutors and light-hearted attempts to guess who the more critical
teachers might be. One boy summed up the feeling of the group
when he remarked that it was interesting "to see ourselves as
others see us." It was becoming increasingly clear that the youngsters were beginning to appreciate the fact that people often saw
them differently from the way they saw themselves, and that it
would be necessary to discover which view, if either, was the
nearer to the truth.

The final technique to which reference will be made here consisted in the application to the groups of the Connolly Occupational
Interests Questionnaire, prepared by Dr Connolly and published
by the Careers Research and Advisory Centre, Cambridge. This
Questionnaire invites the answerer to express preferences between
pairs of activities and occupations and is less unsuitable for children of the ages of those in the groups than might be expected,
since in answering the candidates are asked to ignore the
education, knowledge and ability that they consider might be
necessary for the activities and occupations. In any case the
NFER provides additional instructions and norms for schoolboys
and schoolgirls. Although those children were some years older
than those in our groups, at least some of ours were probably as
mature as many of the older ones.

The Questionnaire is used by the Careers master at Millfield
after a course of training in its use. He felt that at the age of the
children in the groups the main result would be to distinguish
between those boys and girls who were scientifically inclined and
those who were not. From the careers point of view this may be so
with the majority of children, but there are some boys and girls
who have a fairly shrewd notion of their strengths and weaknesses,
and of the main areas of their interests, by the ages of 10, 11 or
12. Indeed, if more attention were paid to this aspect of a child's
life there might be fewer purposeless "children" in our higher educational institutions. However, in our case the main function of
the Questionnaire was to render bright children more knowledgeable about themselves, and it proved a popular and useful means
of achieving this end for most of the pupils concerned.

Before the Questionnaire was presented to the children, they were asked first of all for up-to-date answers to a number of questions. They were invited to state which were their favourite and least liked subjects, giving a reason; for some examples of the kind of job they would like to undertake and some examples of jobs they would hate to have to do. They were then asked to say in which two of seven areas of interests they would like to work and in which two they would not like to work. The seven areas of interests were those covered by the Questionnaire and were dictated from the Handbook with suitable examples of jobs in each area. The areas were, Scientific, Social Service, Persuasive, Literary, Artistic, Recording and dealing with data (called Clerical/Computational), and Practical. When these questions had been answered and checked, the children were given the Questionnaire strictly in accordance with the official instructions. Wherever there was a difficulty, children asked for an explanation and this was provided: with one group the definitions for the various occupations were read out before the Questionnaire was distributed. This procedure is advisable in the case of the younger children. When the forms were completed they were marked by stencil and the results recorded on the front page of the forms. Percentiles were taken from the norms supplied and were recorded as suggested on a fifteen-point literal scale, although most of the children had no difficulty in understanding what is meant by a percentile.

It will probably be most useful to consider two or three individual cases, but there were two general points which are worthy of mention. The first is that the few children who showed no marked interest either positive or negative seemed to be the most immature or those who had little idea of what they were doing in school. The second is that most of the children had correctly forecast at least one of their strengths and one of their weaknesses or dislikes in the questions asked before the distribution of the Questionnaire. There were, however, sufficient discrepancies between the two sets of answers to lead the children to think about themselves.

Girl D claimed that the kind of job she would like would be that of a social worker, or a probation officer, mental health officer or a teacher, while she would not like to be a politician, shopkeeper, factory worker or secretary. Of the seven areas she favoured Social Work or Artistic and did not like Persuasive or Clerical/Computational. On the Questionnaire, her scores for Social Work and Artistic were respectively B and C+, and for Persuasive and Clerical, E and D. She had a B for Literary and for Practical, but she showed little interest in those areas. This girl was one of a small group who sat the Questionnaire again a year later, and it is interesting to notice that Social Service had by then risen to A− and Artistic to B. Literary and Practical had fallen to C, Persuasive D− and Clerical D.

Girl M stated that she would like computer work, accountancy or to be a solicitor, while she would not like to be a teacher, shop-floor worker, or a sales representative. Of the seven areas she favoured Clerical/Computational and Practical, while she did not like Literary or Scientific. Her results showed A− for Clerical and B for Practical. Literary received a D, as did Social Work, but rather surprisingly Scientific was marked B. This girl also filled in the Questionnaire again a year later, and on this occasion Clerical had risen to a full A and Practical to B+; Literary had fallen to E and Persuasive was still in the D category at D+. Scientific still remained at B and she remarked that she must take some account of that fact in her future plans.

Boy P belonged to a younger group but his case is chosen to illustrate the outlook of a more mature child. This boy was under 12 at the time he answered the Questionnaire, and like his regular friend in the class was still rather childish, as, of course, he was still entitled to be. His favourite occupations were those of soccer player, swimmer and disc-jockey and his dislikes, traffic warden, postman and lolly-pop man. Of the seven areas he preferred Literary and Artistic and disliked Scientific and Social Service. His results showed a B− for Artistic and a C for Literary. For Scientific he had a C and for Social Service a B. On being asked to tick those results with which he agreed, he ticked B− for Artistic and C for Scientific, Clerical and Practical. He disagreed with C for Literary and put question marks at B for Social Services and C for Persuasive. This meant that the Questionnaire had at least made him think about himself: it should be interesting to see what will happen if there is an opportunity for him to sit the Questionnaire again.

10

Understanding Others

Some of the exercises described in the previous chapter, while
mainly geared towards self-understanding, were also useful in
directing the attention of the children away from themselves
towards others. For example, the sociometric choices and sociograms brought to their attention the varying degrees of popularity
and the nature of relationships within a class. Moreover, by comparing together the results of the exercises, the pupils would see
for themselves their resemblances and their diversities. This occurred quite clearly with the Study of Values, which thus proved
itself useful in helping the children to understand others. It was
now decided to take another step in this direction by using the
Study to demonstrate to them how little they knew about an adult
with whom they were in frequent contact.

This idea was taken from a doctoral thesis by Dr P. Meldon of
Brentwood College of Education. Dr Meldon had invited some of her
students to fill in the Study as they believed a specified member
of the teaching staff would do: when they had done so, and the
member of staff had obliged by completing the Study, the predictions were compared with the actual answers provided by the
lecturer. The same technique was used by the children at Millfield and Edgarley, who were invited to predict the answers of
one prominent member of staff in each school. The members of
staff then filled in their own answers. The predictions were compared with the actual results: many of the children's estimates
were very wide of the mark but some came quite near. Some
examples are given below. These will be taken from Edgarley where
it was possible to use the Study with more than one group.
The actual scores were as follows:

Theoretical	Economic	Aesthetic	Social	Political	Religious
38	23	24	46	16	33

Here are some of the estimates from a group which had been at the school for at least two years:

M 35	29	18	38	28	32
S 40	28	20	37	37	18
F 33	24	27	41	26	29
J 38	27	18	41	21	41

The range of scores for this group was as follows:

27–42	24–33	18–31	29–41	18–37	18–41

The averages reveal where there was persistent over-stress or under-stress:

36	27	23	38	27	29

In the case of an older group, it was possible to repeat the exercise after a year and so the following examples show both first and second attempts:

	Theoretical	Economic	Aesthetic	Social	Political	Religious
Staff Scores	38	23	24	46	16	33
B (1970)	28	24	17	46	21	44
(1971)	36	25	9	48	22	40
C (1970)	37	28	16	28	31	43
(1971)	40	36	11	36	27	30
D (1970)	29	37	23	45	21	25
(1971)	31	36	20	45	27	21
M (1970)	32	31	18	40	29	30
(1971)	32	29	15	39	24	41

In both sets of scores there is obviously a considerable over-estimate on Political, the average score on that heading being 27 in the first group and 26 in the second. On the whole there was a tendency to over-estimate the Economic and to under-estimate the Social. In both groups Religious showed the widest ranges, although the averages were not far out. Both groups somewhat surprisingly under-estimated the Theroretical although the member of staff was known to be mathematically inclined.

When one compares the estimates made after an interval of a year, one notices that quite a number are the same as the previous ones, or only slightly different. On the other hand, there are some considerable changes as in the case of C in Religious, but this pupil admitted to having vague memories of this from the previous year. M's large increase in Religious occurred because the pupil concerned felt that the teacher was becoming more religious. These discrepancies provided a useful basis for discussion, but not before the children's personal scores had been compared with their estimates for the tutor. It had been thought that at least some of the children might have projected their personal views on to the teacher, but a careful scrutiny of the two sets of scores soon showed conclusively that there was no worthwhile evidence of this in any instance.

In the discussion, the children were asked to consider how far they now thought they really knew the tutor, or those children with whom they were most closely associated in the groups. The answers at first were rather too sweeping, the consensus being that people knew little or nothing about their associates or friends. The pupils were asked to look again at their copies of the Study, and eventually they agreed that they had been right in some particulars about their teacher, and that if they had had to undertake the same exercise on some of their closest friends they would almost certainly have been right in some of their estimates.

In each discussion the children were encouraged to apply what they had learned about themselves and about other pupils to their everyday lives. They were also invited to consider the extent of their understanding of their parents and of their brothers and sisters. They began to suggest that perhaps some of their difficulties at home or in school could have arisen from their lack of knowledge of their parents and teachers. They were asked whether they thought this was a sufficient explanation of difficulties, and whether all they would have to do in the future would be to try to understand other people with whom they lived or worked or played. At first they were inclined to agree. The question was then asked whether this would ensure greater happiness at home and in school. The tendency is for children to assent rather unthinkingly to such a question, but not all of these children did so.

In one group the discussion was widened when a boy remarked that it took two to make a quarrel; in another, a girl suggested that it would be necessary for her older sister to try to understand her, before they would be able to get on better together. The discussion was thus led on to the conclusion that it was necessary in all aspects of life that each human being should try to understand the other people in his environment but that he must also be understood by others.

With the older group (11 to 12+) a reference was made to empathy as a means of understanding others, but these youngsters found it rather difficult to accept the idea of thinking oneself into the attitudes and feelings of another person and at the same time remaining detached. They could appreciate how valuable it would be for a teacher if he could do this in relation to his pupils, but doubted whether any of their own teachers would be able to do it, especially with children, as most must have forgotten what it was like to be children. One boy pointed out that it would be equally impossible for him to do this in relation to a teacher as he had no experience of adult life. This led on to the idea of whether children could ever imagine what their teachers had been like as children, except where teachers had made references to their own childhood. As a result of this discussion it was decided to give some of the children an opportunity to write about some teachers as children.

As the group had an average age of nearly twelve, the children were invited to write about one, two or even three persons as they imagined them to have been at the age of twelve. The three men from whom they could choose were those who had taken the group at some time for experimental purposes. Only a few of the children chose to write about the author, and where one person was chosen this was usually the youngest teacher, who seemed to have a very good relationship with all the children. It was, perhaps, significant that one or two of the boys wrote only a few words on one person and then dried up completely. Others wrote in a rather uninteresting way, primarily because they found little or no challenge in the exercise. One or two were almost certainly on the defensive although they were assured that what they wrote would not be shown to their subjects and that no offence would be taken even if they wrote somewhat facetiously. Samples of each type follow, covering all three people. A refers to the author, and C to the youngest man.

One girl wrote:

> When he was young Mr C was very adventurous. He made a bicycle and he often got into mischief with this bicycle. It had no brakes and the chain kept breaking. He never wanted to help his mother and was always a nuisance around the house. He was always interested in mechanics and would come into the house covered in oil and grease. He once had an alarm clock which was always coming apart and whenever he put it together again it would not work. He would rather play on his own than mix with other people. He often found himself in very difficult scrapes like breaking windows and not being able to pay for new ones. He liked watching trains being overhauled in the nearby railway station.
>
> Before starting and settling down at Edgarley, he was going to be a veterinary surgeon but he did not stay at that job very long because he found that often he had to suffer some very sickening sights. Since he has come to Edgarley he has been a great success.

This girl was content to write about Mr C: she felt she knew too little about the other two men.

A boy wrote:

> By the time he was twelve Mr C was living in Egypt. He was interested in exploration and enjoyed seeing architectural achievements. He saw the Sphinx and the Pyramids. As usual he attempted to climb them, yet in vain for the sun glared down. He attended a private boys' boarding school in Cairo.
>
> About a month after his twelfth birthday he went with the school on a touring holiday by coach around the Mediterranean to France and back. He enjoyed it for he was with friends. He did not exactly enjoy school work although he did like games, especially cricket. He was very curious and enjoyed, when he had the chance, to fiddle with a car-engine. Mechanics were his strong point. He found pleasure from camping, swimming

and fishing. When by the sea he explored the caves and climbed the cliffs. Another speciality was fishing for octopus and catching eels. Apart from the "hatred" of school work he had a high IQ. He was extremely daring and joined in most sports.

Another boy wrote *inter alia* of Mr C, "He used to enjoy the countryside but did not like the towns. I think that he was an all-round 'country-boy.' "

One boy, quite an admirer of Mr C, summed up as follows: "When Mr C grew up he became a teacher and did very well, just from being mischievous like me."

The boy who had written of Mr C as an "all-round 'country-boy' " was one of the few children to attempt to write on all three men, but he had just begun his paragraph on Mr B when time was called. His effort on Mr A was as follows: "When Mr A was twelve he would have a rather quick temper and would find it difficult to understand the others person's point of view. He would find it hard to make friends and indeed would not have many true ones. He did not like sports of any kind. He would be quite good at lessons." He showed some perception here, perhaps from knowing that Mr A had lived and worked in many places, so that deep friendships rarely had time to develop. It is rather ironical to think that Mr A played football, cricket and golf at twelve and later in life was regarded by his wife as "football daft." It is interesting to note that one of the other children to write about Mr A was a girl who imagined him as "an outdoor type."

This girl chose Mr B as the first of her three subjects and wrote of him:

> He attended a grammar school. He was active and good fun. He was rather intelligent and enjoyed outdoor activities. He was popular with the other boys. I think that he might have been a bit of an egg-head. He was clean and reasonably tidy in his appearance. I believe that he might have been cheeky on occasion to the masters and led them on at times.
>
> I don't think that he was particularly good at games but I shouldn't think he slacked. He had a lot of not so deep friendships.

It was interesting to notice that there were very few references to physical characteristics. One boy did refer to Mr A having brown hair and blue eyes. It was true that Mr A had had brown hair which is now mostly grey, but his eyes were and of course still are "green as leeks." Most of the references, however, were either to interests or activities, to which the subjects had probably made reference at times or else they had been observed participating. Several of the references were to relationships and made one wonder whether in fact all the studies of relationships which the children had been making in the experimental work had made them more conscious of the importance of this trait.

Some of the descriptions from the older group were read, but without any mention of names, to a younger group which had also undertaken this exercise. These children were then invited to comment on certain points. They were asked why they thought that some of their older schoolmates had written very little and that usually about one person only. The consensus of answers was that the children concerned were either shy, so that they hesitated to write about their elders, or lacked the imagination to see their elders as they were when children. Two boys maintained that they themselves had been brought up to respect adults, especially teachers, and so they found it very difficult to write on this subject. One girl suggested that in any case the lives of children of the present day are different from those of the children of thirty or forty years ago and so no child of the present day could describe childhood in the past.

They were then asked why they thought that one person had been written about much more than the other two. Most were agreed that this was inevitable since almost all of them had been taught by Mr C and some had even known him as Housemaster. Moreover, he was a friendly person, who sometimes mentioned incidents from his boyhood. As for Mr B, he occupied a more exalted position and was not really so well known as the experiment with the Study of Values had demonstrated. Not only was he less well known, but it was more difficult to imagine him as a boy. Less still was known of Mr A, whom they met once a week and who usually kept them so busy with tests, and so on, that there was little chance of gleaning any autobiographical details. It was obvious that he was a Scotsman from his speech and his dress;

it was clear that he was an academic, since he was referred to as
"Doctor," and an exercise on Africa had revealed that he had
lived in Africa. None of these facts was very helpful in trying to
imagine him as a secondary school pupil.

Finally, the children were asked whether they themselves had
enjoyed the exercise. On the whole, the feeling was hardly favourable, but two or three children declared that they would enjoy it
much more if asked to repeat it. One or two had enjoyed it because
it had given them the chance to be a little facetious. One boy
claimed that he had found it amusing, but what he had done was to
write a brief, slightly humorous description of Mr C, which he had
then repeated verbatim for both Mr A and Mr B. Actually, this was
a sign of development in a very shy boy.

A further attempt to make the children think about and put
themselves in the place of others took the form of writing about
some children in certain photographs. These were of school-children
of about eight to twenty years of age, and College of Education
students, in parts of tropical Africa. The boys were shown in
their uniform of shirt and shorts and the girls normally in frocks.
The Edgarley children were invited to imagine that they were
attending a school in Africa and to describe a school day. Most of
the boys and girls had already heard something from the author
about African schools and children and they had also watched
occasional programmes on television.

It was intended that they should regard themselves as African
pupils and the majority did so, but some merely transferred the
conditions of their own English boarding-school to an African
setting. In this exercise it was noticeable that the more interesting
compositions tended to come from the children who had been
included in the groups for administrative reasons rather than for
outstanding ability. These children seemed to show greater appreciation of the difficulties of some African children in obtaining
entry to a school because of the scarcity of places in some areas.
The boarders seemed to be at an advantage when it came to understanding and sympathizing with feelings of homesickness.
One boy wrote:

I am Noondi and at 13 years old am one of 60 in a school

presided over by Dr B, a psychiatrist. We are wakened at 5 a.m. to a light breakfast of maize and we work then till ten-thirty. We stop then because of the heat of the day. After lunch we lie down and rest till 3 p.m. when we start work again. At 5 p.m. we break up, have tea and go outside to play football. We all have to be in bed by 8 p.m. As I lie in bed I think of my parents almost a thousand miles away in Guinea. I then think of my brothers and sisters and reflect how lucky I was to get here. Just before I go to sleep I think about the next day's school-work, about Maths, English and all the other languages and lessons. And then I am asleep, dreaming pleasant dreams of what I'm going to do at home during the next holidays.

One of the better efforts was written by one of the brightest girls who tended to be rather sensitve about her own feelings and also those of others. She wrote:

We came to school early on a Sunday evening. I was so thankful to have received a place that I did not worry about leaving home. We started to get up at 6.30 the following morn-ing. I was to meet the Head-master after breakfast. I was a little unsure whether I was going to enjoy this. After meeting him I felt more relieved.

We read for a bit before starting at 7.30. We start then so as not to have to work in the heat of the day. The lessons were of a kind that I had not known before, Books were handed out first. There were not many books but to me there seemed hundreds. It seemed an age before lunch but there was not much to eat and it was unpleasantly warm.

Lessons restarted. The other boys seemed cleverer than my-self but I think that was because I was new. The teachers were pretty patient with me but I knew they found me trying. They had a proper gym at the school. I was surprised to see it but we had gym later in the afternoon.

I made friends with a boy older than myself. His name was Kalwindi and he was a year older. At one time I was not listen-ing and I could not find my place in the text but he gave me his book and found the place in mine, then we swopped back again. Kalwindi was very good at running. Late in the evening

I lost my book. Having grown annoyed with it I threw it out of the window in my room. Kalwindi immediately flew out of the door and came back with it. He must have gone tremendously fast.

We were sent to bed early where I thought how my parents and friends would be very proud of me as no-one else had expected me to get to the boarding-school. When the lights were out I was very surprised to hear Kalwindi whisper, because some of the older boys had been telling me of the dreadful things that could happen if you were caught whispering. I whispered this to Kalwindi who told me that the other boys had been teasing me. I felt rather angry but also a little relieved, My first day at my new school had come to an end.

In subsequent discussion the consensus of opinion in all the groups in which this particular exercise was tried was that this was one of the more interesting exercises and certainly to be preferred to the one on the boyhood of members of staff. When reasons were sought for these preferences, most of the children felt that it was easier to write about people whom they did not know personally. They would naturally have less knowledge of such people but this allowed them to use their imagination more freely. When it was pointed out that some of them had not made much use of their imagination and indeed had mainly written about an English school in African conditions, some pleaded in defence that this was the result of their lack of knowledge. It might have been better, they argued, if they had been given more factual details before they had started to write. They still agreed, however, that this was the kind of exercise that they liked.

Of the other techniques used, reference will be made to one only which was a form of a "Guess Who" exercise. There was a twofold purpose in this exercise, firstly to require the children to look at each member of their group, including themselves, and secondly, to make them aware of how they were viewed by the other boys and girls. They were provided with four generalized descriptions and asked to identify the child described in each case. Here is a copy of the sheet with the descriptions and the instructions to the pupils:

Name . . . .

Below are four descriptions of pupils in your group. You are asked to identify the boys and girl and to write their names below each description.

A

This boy has pleasant manners and always seems to have plenty of friends. He likes to be in company and soon grows tired of being alone. He works well in class but is content with doing what he considers to be a reasonable amount of work. He plays games quite well but prefers those with several players on each side.

Name . . . .

B

This girl is hard-working, conscientious and cheerful but she sometimes shows anxiety when she runs up against difficulties. Sometimes she seems to be self-confident and able to fit into any company: occasionally, however, she seems to be rather shy

Name . . . .

C

This boy is well-built and attractive in appearance. Sometimes he seems to be growing up quite quickly but at others he becomes very boyish and juvenile. His school-work is quite well done but he tends, at times, to daydream. He is quite keen on games.

Name . . . .

D

This boy is a natural leader and other boys and girls seem to show respect for him. He accepts this respect but it has not made him conceited. He finds most of his work easy and plays skilfully in many games.

Name . . . .

This exercise was tried with three groups containing respectively 12, 10 and 13 children, the last group being younger than the others by about a year. There was no real problem with the older groups, each of which found quickly a boy who seemed to be described under D. In each case the determining feature was "plays skilfully in several games." In one group all the girls were mentioned by somebody, including one girl who recognized herself, but in the other one girl was not mentioned: she was a girl who did not show shyness on any occasion. In both groups the boys, other than the outstanding D's, were mentioned, but in one group one boy had seven references, five under A, and one each under C and D. It is interesting to observe that he identified himself in A.

In subsequent discussion, the children were told that the descriptions had been of a general nature and that they had actually been used in two groups. Both groups felt that this might be true of A, B and C, but that the person who made up the descriptions must have had some boy in mind for D. The author had to admit that in the construction of these descriptions, which had to have some degree of suitability for the subjects, it was difficult to be completely objective. In some cases devisers undoubtedly had some person in mind but they then added other characteristics to make the descriptions more general. When the exercise was intended for a large number of people, this might not matter, but it did seem to matter within a small group.

When these groups were asked if they could see any other difficulties in the construction of these exercises, they rapidly pointed out some that had occurred to them. There was obviously a limitation, where a small group was involved, on the inclusion of physical features such as height, features, colour of eyes, colour of hair and so on. There was the same limitation on dress. One of the two boys in a group wearing short trousers pointed out that if shorts had been mentioned everyone would have chosen him or the other boy, hence a reference to a specific subject, game or hobby would be likely to lead to one boy or girl being chosen. As the children considered these difficulties, they seemed to realize that it was all the more remarkable that some of them were able to recognize themselves. Two or three of the pupils thought that it would be better to make the descriptions longer with more items: they felt that this would make them look at each other more carefully.

When the third group was invited to complete the form, it was noticeable that there was a good deal of hesitation and the children had to be given some encouragement to go on. They ultimately did so, but in two or three cases children could be observed changing their minds and scoring out the names that they had already inserted. Two of the boys (there were nine boys and four girls in the group) protested that they could not find a fourth person for D, but they were persuaded to try again and they then used the name of a boy for the second time.

This result seemed to be interesting enough to justify the drawing up of a table, which is given here. The boys are numbered from 1 to 9 and the girls from 10 to 13.

Pupils Identified

Pupil	A	B	C	D	
1	8	11	7	5	
2	5	13	6	4	
3	5	13	9	5	Same boy in A and D. (Not mentioned by anyone)
4	6	12	8	7	
5	5	13	6	4	Self-recognition
6	4	13	1	7	
7	7	10	5	9	Self-recognition
8	5	12	1	7	
9	5	12	7	5	Same boy in A and D.
10	5	13	6	7	
11	2	11	1	8	Self-recognition
12	2	10	4	7	
13	7	10	1	8	

Pupils making Identification

Summary of Number of Times Identified

1	4C	8	1A, 1C, 2D
2	2A	9	1C, 1D
3	Nil	10	3B
4	1A, 1C, 2D	11	2B
5	6A, 1C, 3D	12	3B
6	1A, 3C	13	5B
7	2A, 2C, 5D		

As the descriptions had been devised for the older groups, there was no possibility in this group that the author had had any of the boys or girls in mind. In the discussion, however, another criticism was voiced, namely that some of the difficulties had arisen from the fact that on the whole the children were not very keen on games. Even those who liked games tended to restrict their interest to one or two sports. The conclusion of the group was that anyone making up such descriptions required, firstly, a greater knowledge of the members, and secondly, a bias towards the more general interests of the group members.

When they were presented with a summary of the results, with figures in place of names, they noted first of all that although one girl had been identified five times, all four girls had been named. They thought that this showed a remarkable result. When they observed that four of the boys had been identified under A, C and D, they were divided in their view. A few felt that this was a good sign and that those cases where boys were identified chiefly under one heading were not general enough. Others took the view that the descriptions of the boys were in some ways too much alike. This view was supported by the two boys who had identified the same boy under A and D: they maintained that the two descriptions were quite comparable.

Two other points of interest were brought out in the discussion. The first of these was that only one person, a boy, had not been identified by anyone, nor even by his desk companion, whom he had named and with whom he often collaborated in work, sometimes despite an appeal for strictly individual work. It was agreed that he must have a distinctive character not covered by any of the descriptions. As he was one of those of above average popularity in the sociogram for the group, this seemed the most likely explanation. The other point was that one of the boys who recognized himself under A was recognized by only one other pupil under that heading, whereas two boys recognized his description in C and three boys and two girls were sure he was described under D. Such other evidence as existed suggested that he was an unlikely D. For example, on the sociogram, from which group leaders were to be chosen, he was chosen by only two boys. He was liked but hardly respected by the majority of the group.

As reference has been made to the sociogram, it may be of interest to the reader to compare a summary of the results of the sociometric test, which was on a criterion of work, with the table given below. It will be recalled that the children made their first choices, as shown in Column X, without instructions that the groups had to contain boys and girls, and their second choices, as shown in Column Y, after that instruction had been given.

Child	X		Y	
	Chosen by		Chosen by	
	Boys	Girls	Boys	Girls
1	6	0	3	1
2	6	0	5	2
3	5	0	2	2
4	1	0	0	1
5	6	0	5	3
6	1	0	1	0
7	1	0	2	0
8	1	0	0	0
9	0	0	0	0
10	0	3	3	2
11	0	3	3	0
12	0	3	0	1
13	0	3	3	0

11
Case Studies

So far we have placed much of the emphasis on the procedures in class leading to a knowledge of gifted children as a group. Samples of the work done have been used to throw a fairly general light on the children, but none has been considered as an individual. In the present chapter there are four case studies, three boys and one girl, and it is hoped that these will serve two purposes. The first of these is to give the reader an opportunity of looking at the profiles of some of the individual children from early childhood. The second is to bring the results of the various tests together in a number of cases and so illustrate the experimental work from the viewpoints of a number of individuals.

When it became evident that case studies would be worth while, it was decided to restrict these to children at Edgarley, partly for administrative reasons and partly because some of the children would be available for further study before being transferred to the senior school. The Headmaster was asked to choose a number of children whose parents would be available and likely to respond. A letter was sent to these parents, all of whom replied that they would be willing to provide information about the earlier years of their children. When the replies had been received, the author sent the Questionnaire printed below, together with a covering letter inviting the parents to complete it as far as they could. It was suggested that question 27 might well prove to be the most useful and it is interesting to note that most of the parents responded very well to this question, providing much valuable information. In the letter, the hope was expressed that the parents might enjoy the task set, and some parents admitted, when they returned the completed forms, that they had found pleasure in it.

The Questionnaire was as follows:

Questionnaire on Special Groups

1 Full name of child ....
2 Date and place of birth ....
3 Number of older brothers and sisters ....
4 Number of younger brothers and sisters ....
5 Age at which he/she first sat up ....
6 Age at which he/she first crawled ....
7 Age at which he/she first walked ....
8 Age at which he/she first talked ....
9 Favourite playthings or toys at various ages. Please give
   details ....
   ....
10 When did frequent questions start? ....
11 Did he/she read before attending school? ....
   At what age? ....
12 Age of first going to
       (*a*) kindergarten or nursery school ....
       (*b*) infants school ....
13 Any liking for long words? If so at what age? ....
14 Did he/she show favourable attitudes, about age 6–7, to
       (*a*) parents...............................
       (*b*) brothers and sisters ....
       (*c*) school ....
       (*d*) companions at play ....
15 Does he/she now show favourable attitudes towards
       (*a*) parents ....
       (*b*) brothers and sisters ....
       (*c*) school ....
       (*d*) companions at play ....
16 In which countries has he/she lived for at least a year? ...
   ....
17 Childhood diseases suffered from? ....
   At what ages ....
18 What is his/her general behaviour at home now? ....

19   Has he/she ever appeared older than his/her actual years?
          . If so at what age or ages? . . . .

20   Were there any times when there was a clear disparity between the intellectual development and the physical, emotional and social development? . . . .

21   Was he/she read stories in childhood? . . . .

22   Could he/she tell the time before going to school? . . . . . .

23   Did he/she show any signs of giftedness in the infants
school? . . . .

24   Does he/she show any signs of giftedness now? . . . .

25   Do you have the results of any test (e.g. an intelligence
test) for him or her? If so please give them stating the name
of the test if possible . . . .
. . . .

26   Do you have any similar test results for his/her brothers
and sisters? If so please give them . . . .
. . . .

27   Please give any further relevant material or information
about your child, mentioning any interesting points about
his/her intelligence or other giftedness.

Before dealing with individual cases, there are some general
points arising from the completed forms. One of these is that the
majority of the children had learned to read before the age of five,
and some actually before the age of four. Secondly, there was a
tendency for these children to assume, when they began to attend
school, that they were the normal children, so that they were
puzzled by the fact that the majority of their class-mates were
still unable to read. Some were promoted early but most had out-
stripped the facilities offered by their schools and had been tested
by a psychologist. The parents had then been advised to consider
Millfield or Edgarley. Several of the parents felt that Edgarley had
been beneficial to their children but in one or two cases problems
remained to be solved. Most parents maintained that their children's attitudes to them were favourable but they also noticed the
tendency of their offspring to grow away from them and to develop
the normal teenage attitudes.

Most of the children had suffered from one or more of the

ordinary childhood ailments but they were on the whole a healthy sample of the population. Such problems as had occurred had arisen from boredom and lack of challenge at school or from the uneven development of their intellect, emotions and physique. In several cases the parents were aware of their children's IQ, although they might not know the actual figure, as psychologists are reluctant to disclose this to parents. The majority knew that their children were gifted to some extent but some preferred the term "bright," feeling that "gifted" was too high a term for their child. The parents of one child knew that their boy was of superior quality but much of his school-work suggested that he was not. These parents were relieved that their younger children had not been tested and hoped that they would not be: the knowledge of their son's ability had merely intensified their problems with him. Finally, the parents in each completed questionnaire seemed to have made the attempt to be as objective as possible, and where they could not answer satisfactorily they had left the question unanswered. This fact should render the case studies which follow more useful and more reliable.

A, who was born in 1960, began to walk at about 10 months and he was talking by the age of 14 months. From the age of about two years he has shown an interest in working models and also in books, which he was beginning to read from about 4¼ years. Persistent questioning dates from his acquisition of speech. He first went to school at the age of 5, and was sometimes bored, as he was already reading and much ahead of his class-mates. By the age of 7 he had an extensive vocabulary including a number of long words. Apart from two of the common childhood complaints he has always enjoyed good health and although small is always energetic in activities in which he is interested. An only child, he has been friendly at home, but when he was younger his attitude to school companions was not always favourable: this seems to have improved at Edgarley. He has always seemed rather older than his years, has shown some signs of giftedness throughout, and has always had a passion for knowing and acquiring facts. His IQ, taken by an experienced psychologist, was 148 on the WISC. In the AH4 test at Edgarley he had a score of $2 \cdot 3\sigma$ amongst children of his own age.

His approach to study seems to be factual. There was an exercise on "A Day at School" for which he produced a timetable of his normal school day, and another exercise on the advice he would give to a child about to come to boarding-school for the first time, for which he produced a collection of instructions of the kind of: "Don't be cheeky to teachers." In the story-completion exercises he did not show much imagination but he wrote practically with a good deal of common sense. In the Creativity exercises he had modest scores on Thinking Creatively with Pictures at 9·5 but he showed some development by 11·6 especially in the treatment of the third exercise. At 9·2 his essay on "The Cat that Talks" was technically competent but not very interesting.

In the Study of Values he was above average on Theoretical, Economic and Political, was average on Aesthetic and Social and well below average on Religious. In Music he has a great preference for "pop."

On the 16PF profile he agreed with the conclusions of the test that he is affected by his feelings, is assertive, conscientious, shy, suspicious, apprehensive, self-sufficient and tense, but he disagreed with the implications that he is about average on warm-heartedness, intelligence, and tough-tender-minded. In the Myers–Brigg type of test he showed himself to be rather shy and introverted, with some bias towards the abstract but with a preference also for common sense over imagination. He underlined the statement that he had a lot of worries, and this agrees with some of the factors in the 16PF profile. It is interesting to note that on the "Guess Who" type test he changed the name he had written in for A and inserted his own name instead.

In the Sentence Completion exercise he expressed a desire to play for a first league football club and to enter the Royal Navy. He confessed that he sometimes regarded himself as "silly." In his relationship with other people he felt that his teachers sometimes regarded him as cheeky but that most adults believed that he acted above his chronological age. Actually, the verdict of his teachers was that he is reserved, affected by his feelings, usually obedient, serious, shy, apprehensive, controlled and tense.

In the Connolly Occupational Interests Questionnaire preliminary study he stated that he liked best Scientific and Practical and that he liked least Persuasive and Artistic. In 1971 his scores for Scientific and Practical were respectively A— and C, and for Persuasive and Artistic D and E. He had B for Social Service and for Clerical/Computational. In 1972 he had A— and C again for Scientific and Practical, and D and E for persuasive and Artistic. Although Clerical/Computational remained at B, Social Service had fallen to C.

B, a boy born in 1960, had been able to sit up at the age of 5½ months, had begun crawling at about 7 months and walking at about 13 months. He had a fair vocabulary, consisting mostly of nouns, by 15 months, and was quite fluent by the age of 2 years. The stage of frequent and persistent questions dated from the latter part of his third year. He showed no exclusive interest in any one kind of toy, but would play readily with whatever was available. He began to pick up reading at about 3½ years and was a good reader before he went to school at the age of 5 years. He showed from early life a partiality for long words: some of these were his own coinages. In his days in the infant school his attitude to his parents and two older brothers was reasonably favourable, but he tended to be rather condescending to some of his classmates. In more recent years his attitude to his parents has varied considerably according to circumstances and to his moods. As the youngest of three boys, all bright, he has frequently resented the patronizing approach to himself as the "baby" of the family, and at one stage expressed a preference for school over home, since at school he was free from their influence and presence. In a brief autobiographical sketch, written when he was 11 years old, he concluded, "I am thought very funny and cute which I *don't* like."

At the time of writing, this boy is approaching his teens, and he seems more settled, outwardly at least: his membership of the special group may have contributed. At his boarding-school he has some friends, but he has, naturally enough, very few at home. He has always enjoyed good health and has suffered from hardly any of the common children's diseases.

With an IQ of 154 on the WISC, it is not surprising that he has often seemed intellectually in advance of his chronological age, but in social and physical development he would rank about average for his age-group. The disparity between his intellectual and other forms of development showed up most clearly at the time that he felt himself patronized by his brothers. In intellectual activities his brothers have tended to be relatively specific, but B, with a very high potential, has been more generalized in his. He has responded so far better in the literary than in the mathematical aspects of school-work. In relation to other children he seems to have the ability to understand the motivation behind their behaviour, but like many other high IQ children he appears at times to lack a thoughful sympathy and there is little evidence of empathy. Nevertheless, he is capable of leadership but only when he feels the urge to lead.

The reference above to his being thought very funny may have arisen from his frequent approach to matters in a flippant way: at times he seems determined to be amusing whatever the circumstances. Thus it was B who wrote the Wellsian type of account of the boy who had lost his memory (Chapter 8). In the other Story Completion exercise on Justin and his failure at sports, he finished up with Justin drowning himself and Justin's father dying of grief on hearing the sad news. One inevitably wonders whether a boy who writes in this way regularly has some deep problem which he has been unable to solve, or whether he is writing with his tongue in his cheek. Again, in the story of Oswald who performs so poorly in his first year at a secondary school, Oswald discovers a fire in which fifteen people perish but many are saved because Oswald gave the alarm. When some people come to thank Oswald, he is not available as he was one of the fifteen killed. B actually describes Oswald as "paranoiac." In this grim, unlikely story one hears echoes of Saki, but the tone of the story is more akin to Lewis Carroll's "Walrus and the Carpenter": "And answer came there none."

In the four stories based on projective-type pictures were echoes of Ambrose Bierce, one of whose stories had been read to the group and had been much appreciated by B. However, while the endings of the stories were given in the Bierce tradition the style of the stories was not: it was more like that of Saki's *Reginald*.

In the 16PF Test Profile, B had high scores on Suspicions and Self-opinionated, Tense, Forthright and Follows own Urges. He disagreed about being forthright but accepted that he was about half way between self-assured and apprehensive, that he followed his own urges and that he was rather more group-dependent than self-sufficient.

In the Sentence Completion Test he showed signs of independence and of self-criticism. He gave evidence of a favourable attitude towards his parents but seemed to feel some guilt about his attitude and behaviour towards his brothers. His liking for football manifested itself wherever possible. One completion which had been changed half way through may have had some significance. To the words, "I feel that my family thinks me" he had begun to add the word "unbearable," but this was scored through and the words, "a normal boy" substituted.

In the Myers—Brigg type of test he showed a preference for firmness and decisiveness. The test provides evidence of his liking for people and of his feeling that he can mix readily with other children. He supported common sense rather than imagination. It was a little surprising to find that he was one of the majority of the children who agreed that the life of a child is more interesting than that of an adult.

While his relationships with children were reasonably good, as the group sociogram demonstrated, those with his tutors were often short of perfection. His tutors generally agreed that B tends to be reserved, that he is rather easily affected by his feelings, that he is excitable, assertive, usually obedient but likely to disregard rules, fond of group activity, and self-assured. The somewhat unexpected comment from most of his teachers was that his thought is characterized by concrete rather than abstract thinking. In the reasoning exercises and in the WISC, B had displayed a considerable talent for abstract thinking. When filling in his own version of the pro-forma issued to teachers, B underlined abstract thinking. Perhaps his teachers' attitude will be more easily understood and appreciated when we consider the reaction of B when he learned that he might appear as a "case," albeit anonymously, in a book. Immediately, he remarked: "I shall expect a high fee for that!" One or two of the other children expressed the view that it would be an honour to appear in a book and that a boy so honoured ought not to be so mercenary. B disagreed with this viewpoint.

In the Study of Values, at the age of ten, he was well above average on Economic (not surprising after his request for a fee), just above average on Theoretical and Aesthetic, below average on Social and Political, and well below average on Religious. Eighteen months later he was still well above average on Economic, just above average on Social and Political, average on Theoretical and Aesthetic and still further below average on Religious. In assessing the member of staff he slightly over-estimated on Theoretical and slightly underestimated on Religious. He was much too high on Economic and Political and much too low on Aesthetic and Social.

In the field of Creativity his essay on "The Cat that Talks" was undistinguished except for the stress on the success of the cat in economic affairs. In Thinking Creatively with Words, his Fluency was above average but his Originality was about average for his Edgarley age-group. In Thinking Creatively with Pictures, at the age of ten, he had modest scores for Fluency, Flexibility and Originality. In 1972, at the age of twelve, he revealed a considerable development, especially in the originality of his drawings.

In the Connolly Occupational Interests Questionnaire, at the age of eleven, he had an A on Literary (his favourite subject at the time was English), C+ on Aesthetic and C on Scientific, Social Welfare, Persuasive and Practical, and D on Clerical/Computational. In the following year, Literary had fallen from A to B, while Social Welfare had risen from C to B+. Persuasive now stood at C+ while Scientific and Aesthetic each had C. Clerical/Computational had improved slightly from D to C−, but Practical had fallen from C to D. It seems reasonably certain that this boy will maintain his interest in the Literary field. The greater interest in the Social Welfare may prove to be transient, but it is just as likely that it is a welcome sign of social motivation. A little light may be thrown on this by his answer to the question as to which jobs he would most like to undertake as an adult, which was: Professional Footballer, English Tutor, and Journalist. When asked which school subjects he most enjoyed, and why, his response was:

Chemistry: exciting at times and interesting; a humorous tutor.
English: good fun.
Latin: I like translating it.

The most notable of the jobs which he would not like to undertake was Prime Minister.

C, a girl, born in 1960, did not score as highly on the individual intelligence test as A or B, her full score being 133 on the WISC, the performance score being well under the verbal score. She is, however, a girl of talent, whose career shows many of the characteristics of the gifted child. For example, when she was about 2½ years, her best friend, a 4-year-old girl, began to attend a nursery school and so C was deprived of much of her companionship. C was keen to go to the nursery school, which admitted children at 4 years. Her parents explained to her that she could not go to school until she was able to read and write. A few months later, to the discomfort of the parents, C had acquired these arts and demanded to be sent to the nursery school to join her friend. By dint of much persuasion the Head of the school agreed to admit her.

She had been talking from about a year old, and soon began to show a liking for quite long words. She was brought up in a household where the parents never talked down to her. At the infant school stage her attitudes to her parents and baby brother were favourable, but she sometimes betrayed some irritation with slower children and tended to form friendships with older children. Her favourable attitudes to her parents have been maintained and she appears to put up with her younger brother with a kind of amused tolerance. Her friendships still tend to be with children older than herself. The sociogram suggests that her coevals find her rather mature for them. In the "Guess Who" type test, three boys identified her as the girl described.

Other signs of precocity were her beginning to learn chess at about four years, her keeping of a travel-diary on a trip to Venice at 5½ years, her acquisition of some swimming medals by the age of eight, and her being promoted to the top group in her village school by the time she was eight years old. It is not surprising that she usually made friends with older children. After testing by a local psychologist, she was sent to Edgarley, where the challenge was likely to be greater than in the village school, although she received there much help and consideration.

Another common characteristic of very bright children is their capacity to exist on a minimum of sleep, and C, at least at home, sleeps well under the average for children of her age.

In the 16PF Test Profile the qualities which showed up most distinctly were Happy-go-lucky, Conscientious, Self-reliant, Forthright, Apprehensive, Liberal, and Tense. C agreed with most of the test results, but disagreed with Self-Reliant and Liberal.

In the Myers—Brigg type test she revealed a strong preference for ideas, inventions, and imagination. She favoured a few close friendships rather than a wide circle of acquaintances. Like the majority in her group, she felt that a child's life is more interesting than that of an adult. She claimed to have very few worries.

In the Study of Values she was in the top 10 per cent for Theoretical, above average on Aesthetic, average on Economic and Political, below average on Social and in the lowest 10 per cent for Religious. In predicting the scores for the member of staff she was nearly right on Theoretical, Economic and Religious, too high on Aesthetic and Political and well below on Social. Apart from Religious, her own categories were much the same as those she had predicted for the master.

C's only Story Completion was that of the boy who had lost his memory. According to her, this had happened as the result of an air crash in which the boy and an air-hostess had been the only survivors. The air-hostess had taken him to his home area. Eventually he recovered his memory through seeing, in the furniture shop, an old chest which he knew and which bore the inscription, "He to whose family this chest belongs will lose his memory in the seventeenth century before the end of the world." The eleven child-critics gave C three a's, five b's and three c's for Originality, five b's and six c's for Relevance, and two a's, three b's and six c's for interest.

In Creativity, C had shown a keen sense of humour in her essay on "The Monkey that Flies," in which she introduced into the jungle a hat salesman, from whom the monkey stole an orange-coloured hat. In Thinking Creatively with Pictures her scores for Fluency, Flexibility and Originality were about average for her group. These tests gave little opportunity for showing her skill with her hands: three of her favourite subjects are Art, Needlework and Creative Design.

In the projective-type pictures exercise, her two stories on pictures based on children's relationships with each other were about children quarrelling: in one of them a boy began to strangle his brother. The two dealing with adult-child relationships were hardly any happier.

Before filling in the Connolly Occupational Interests Questionnaire, C stated that her preferences were for Scientific and Aesthetic and that her dislikes were Social Welfare and Literary. Her actual results were a B for Scientific, an A for Aesthetic, a B+ for Practical, a C for Persuasive and Literary, and a D for Social Welfare and for Clerical/Computational. She seemed surprised by the B+ for Practical, but she is in fact, despite her marked preference for Theoretical in the Study of Values, interested in practical activities.

D, a boy, was born in 1959, and was able to sit up unaided by five months. Crawling began at six months and walking, with the help of the furniture, at about seven months. By eighteen months D had a vocabulary of 35 words, and by twenty-one months, one of 250 words. The parents kept notes on him because he was the first child. His favourite playthings were toy animals which were cast as characters in various forms of dramatic play. With the development of speech came the usual frequent questions. D learned to read about the age of four years, at which age he began to attend a nursery school. He was less concerned with the use of long words than with choosing the precise word, and this has led sometimes to his saying nothing in preference to using an inexact expression. He began to learn chess about the age of five years.

At the infant school stage his attitudes to his parents were favourable but were less so to his younger sisters. He did not like school but he was friendly towards his companions at play. His attitudes at present are favourable to his parents, sisters and companions, but his attitude to school is ambivalent. He has had some of the usual illnesses of childhood, the last being at the age of twelve.

D is an example of a child whose intellectual, emotional and social ages are widely different. Intellectually he is capable of adult levels of thought in certain fields, His WISC score was 142. Emotionally he is still quite young and tends to over-react in success and failure, He expects a good deal of attention and is upset if he does not receive it. In school he makes little approach to those who could help him: indeed, those who are most willing to help find it difficult to do so because of his tendency to regress. There are some signs of maturation, and the disparities in the various ages are lessening: they are still, however, a handicap in his academic and social life. His physical skills are not greatly developed and this shows up in his handwriting, which is poor and sometimes difficult to read. Like many other gifted children he is disinclined to commit himself on paper: in any case, his search for the right word seems to handicap him in composition.

About the age of six, D developed an interest in Astronomy, and somewhat later in Zoology and Prehistoric life. This interest in certain scientific fields has been active, as when, at the age of eight, he read about the "lost" moon of Saturn, which he thought was probably Pluto. He wrote to Mr Patrick Moore about this and, despite the scrawled letter, received a courteous reply setting out several reasons why Pluto could not be the lost moon. Some of his questions at school on scientific matters have been misunderstood or else have proved beyond the immediate knowledge of some of his teachers. Unfortunately much of his ordinary schoolwork has been at best undistinguished, so that his teachers have found it hard to discover evidence of giftedness. It is hardly the fault of his teachers if they have under-estimated some of his powers. In a statement at the age of twelve he mentioned that his favourite studies were Astronomy and Nuclear Physics.

At the age of 10.5 his score on the AH4 was 64. He was rather slow in answering for a boy of his age and ability. In the first section he answered 29 items with only two errors. In the second part he answered 44 items with 7 errors. This was satisfactory, but was not much above the average for the whole age-group sitting the test. His WISC score was very good, but his scores varied considerably on the various sub-tests.

In the 16PF Test Profile he showed very highly on Tender-minded, Clinging, Shrewd and Self-sufficient, and Highly on Experimenting, Tense, Controlled, Suspicious and Imaginative. His only score on the Low Score side was Sober, Serious, with which he disagreed.

He disagreed also with Tender-minded but accepted Suspicious, Experimenting, Self-sufficient, and Tense. He expressed no opinion on the others.

In the Story Completion Test on the boy who had lost his memory, he painted a most desolate scene with the boy lost, suffering excruciating pain and bleeding from a stab-wound. He expressed the sense of pain very vividly and also the feeling of pained puzzlement:

> Seventeen what did it mean? Did it mean pain or what? he saw a group of about 16 boys or well about about 16.

Actually, it is difficult in this instance to say whether the repetitions are "careless," or whether in fact the young author has an empathic understanding of a boy in such a situation. The young critics who assessed these essays, without knowing the name of the author, awarded no a's. They gave four b's and six c's for Originality, four b's and six c's for Relevance and one b and nine c's for Interest.

In Creativity, in the essay on "The Lion who couldn't Roar," his scores for all aspects were c, except for Humour, where it was b. The essay was not starred by Mr Moir. D describes how the lion constantly forgot how to roar and how in certain circumstances he had recourse to a dictionary, which referred him to growling, which he then had to look up. On one occasion he used a Zebra dictionary, but it was merely a translation into Zebra of the dictionary which he had used previously, On another occasion the lion consulted the Flying Monkey and the Cat that Talked. In Thinking Creatively with Pictures, D's scores were well above average.

In the projective-pictures type of test, he wrote in much the same way as he had done in his story of the lost boy. In the case of the picture showing two figures approaching a hole, the boy called out to his father that he could not go on as something was overwhelming him. But this fear was overcome and this was a victory for the boy. Then he looked into the hole and it was as if his head flew off his body. In a second story, a father is telling his daughter to come down from a height and the daughter is refusing. This story was a dialogue, as was the third, which concerned an accident to a girl and the summoning of a doctor. The final story was about a boy looking over a fence to watch his favourite football team.

In the Connolly Occupational Interests Questionnaire, his high scores were B+ for Scientific and B for Clerical/Computational. For Social Welfare and Practical the score was C−, and for Persuasive, Literary, and Aesthetic the score was C. This seems to be a pretty accurate assessment and these two interests are likely to persist. It would seem that if full contact is to be established with D in the academic and social fields, the approach will have to be made through these two interests.

12

Conclusions

One definite conclusion which can be drawn from the studies at
Millfield and Edgarley is that a considerable number of gifted
children are under-achieving. In some case it is clear to the teachers
that the children are capable of a higher standard of work but
these teachers may not always be able to provide the necessary
additional stimulus until the children overcome the hampering
effects of the concept of "the stint." In schools where there are
large classes this is an exceedingly difficult task and in large classes
with a wide range of ability it is probably an impossible undertaking.

In other instances teachers are unaware of the full potential-
ities of the more gifted children, either because the children are
highly successful in playing down their abilities for social or other
reasons or else because they obtain consistently high marks in the
teacher's subject or subjects. When a child receives, time after time,
marks of 85 to 100 per cent in a subject, there is a strong presump-
tion that the work is on the easy side for that child and, in consequence, the boy or girl is probably under-achieving. Ultimately,
such children may reach such a stage of conditioning that they
believe they are performing very well and nothing more is required.
In discussion some of the Millfield and Edgarley children admitted
that they were not making any attempt to reach the standards of
which they felt themselves capable: they were content instead to
do well just what they were set. Others showed less awareness, but
once the possibility that high marks might be linked with too low
a standard of work was pointed out to them, they agreed that
they had not really been exerting themselves.

One factor, then, in under-achievement is frequently a low level
of aspiration. This may arise from parental, school or pupil atti-

tudes or from a combination of them. Many parents, teachers and pupils are content to set their sights on some examination which may present too low or too limited a target. The stint becomes in effect a sufficiency of work at a suitable level to pass the particular examination and quite often activities not immediately connected with the examination tend to be neglected or ignored. On the whole, the low level of aspiration is seen in the field of creative work, but even in the more academic aspects of education it is often consistently low.

Problems arising from giftedness in children are often further complicated for parents who have other somewhat less gifted children to cater for. The more perceptive parents can observe the strains and stresses which may develop in a household and may endeavour to avoid unpleasantness or ill-feeling by a series of balances within the family relationships. In those instances where they are most successful in keeping the peace they may unwittingly encourage their gifted child or children to underplay their gifts. In other instances parents have to face up to the difficult problem of bringing up a gifted child whose intellectual, emotional and social development may be unbalanced. In such cases it is tempting to play down the intellectual development. Teachers have to deal with groups or classes of children of varying abilities and varying developments and so may find themselves solving some of their problems by under-valuing the abilities of the more gifted children.

The evidence arising from this study suggests that there are certain needs which apply to some gifted and others which may apply to all gifted children. These needs are not exclusive to gifted children but are often most manifest in such children.

The first of those needs is a higher level of aspiration on the part of parents, teachers and the children themselves in areas in which the children are gifted. This necessitates a greater understanding by parents of their own children and of their capacities. In most cases it requires the parents to realize that their children have weaknesses as well as strengths. In pre-school days it calls for closer observation by the parents and, after the children begin to attend school, regular liaison between parents and teachers. A high standard of performance must be expected and encouraged both at home and in school. On the other hand parents and teachers must be careful to avoid excessive expectations. Some teachers must be willing to revise their attitudes towards the more gifted and to make a real effort to devise work for them which will prove an adequate challenge and not just satisfy the stint.

Some of the children must also alter a number of their attitudes. They must be made aware of the existence of the stint in their approach to school and other work. They must also be helped to a revised estimate of their own abilities. Those who over-estimate their abilities in any area have to be made conscious of this, while those who under-estimate their powers have to be made to understand that in certain areas they are capable of a higher standard of performance. A fresh view of their aims or targets is called for, and they should be led to understand that while they have to pass certain examinations, largely because of our social system, such examinations are incidental and are to be passed without an excess of effort. Their real effort is to be devoted rather to achieving a much higher standard than is required in passing the normal examinations.

Gifted, and indeed all children, should be made to realize that activities of a creative or divergent nature are just as important in life as those of a more closed or convergent nature. If a boy or girl has some creative ability it should be regarded as much as a gift as is high academic ability. The idea that these activities, unlike Mathematics and Science, are not of great importance, and so do not call for a high effort or standard of performance, must be changed. If it is not changed, some youngsters will not develop part of their talent and the lack of effort in one field may soon spread to all the acivities of the children concerned[1]. The performance of several of the pupils studied at Millfield and Edgarley was particularly disappointing on the literary side, so much so that a few of them were, in a sense, handicapped children, because they lacked a satisfactory means of expressing their often quite abundant ideas. Others again had been influenced by the common belief, repeated in their homes, that mathematical studies are

[1] This probably explains why some gifted children seem to "burn out" in the Secondary school.

especially difficult for girls, so that a phobia reinforced the low
level of aspiration. Parents and teachers must be on their guard
against creating or strengthening such fears, or justifications for
poor performances.

Another need which has manifested itself is that of self-understanding, a need for all children before they reach adult status
and responsibilities, but one which is often dealt with inadequately.
This does not mean that each child should be encouraged to spend
a good deal of his time in contemplation or introspection, valuable
as these activities may be to all mankind. It does mean, however,
that they should at least have some perception of their own beliefs,
prejudices, habits, attitudes and capabilities. Such knowledge of
oneself is usually acquired gradually and very imperfectly, but
there seems to be no reason against the process being rendered
more systematic so that children may be more skilled in piecing
together the various elements in their experience. The second
implication of self-understanding is that one should become more
conscious of how one is regarded by others — a gift, as Robert
Burns points out in his poem, "To a Louse." The process may
involve a certain amount of pain and upset to the person concerned
but the price is probably trifling compared with the hurt that one
can inflict on others as well as on oneself because of a lack of self-
understanding. One of the other advantages of an increase in self-
understanding is that one can begin to develop a greater understanding of other people and so some of the verdicts of other
people on oneself may be rendered more acceptable and therefore
more valuable.

A great need of all children, and also of all adults, is this greater
understanding of other people so that there may be an improvement in their relationships with others. With gifted children we
have observed problems in their relationships with parents,
brothers and sisters, teachers, and also with other children. In a
number of cases more than one of these relationships may be a
source of trouble. Whether all children are capable of understanding those relationships through their own efforts or by empathy
is uncertain. What does seem certain is that children can be helped
to understand others better after they have begun to understand
themselves. Parents and teachers can help, when they have them-

selves made sufficient advancement in the art of understanding others, by trying to show children how they stand in relation to others. If they can demonstrate to their children how they them- selves react to the actions and opinions of others, they can bring the children to see how and why others react to them in the way they do.

One purpose of the study of gifted children at Millfield and Edgarley has been to discover some of their needs, but another has been to explore ways and means of meeting those needs. Inevitably in the course of experimental work one finds that certain techniques produce little result while others prove more fruitful. In the same way, at these two schools, some techniques proved more stimulating and interesting to the children than others. The suggestions which follow are based largely on those techniques which the children themselves preferred.

While there is no overwhelming evidence in favour of special schools or even special classes for gifted children, there is con- vincing evidence that such children can benefit from spending at least part of their time in the presence of children of about their own level of ability. Such peer groups can take the form of a club meeting regularly, or they can meet at times allocated on the school timetable. Whether as a class or group or club, the person in charge can be a member of staff, preferably one who has made some special study of the problems of gifted children during his professional training, or he can be a Head teacher, if suitably qualified, or a peripatetic teacher, who might also help with some of the slow learners. In an area where numbers are small, the child- ren can be brought together for a half or a whole day in some centrally placed school or other educational institution, such as a College of Education. This last type of arrangement is already to be found in Essex, West Sussex, Bristol, and some other places.

It has been stressed that gifted children often gain considerably from contact with intelligent, stimulating and knowledgeable adults in addition to their regular teachers. Where the children are normally in large classes, the greater is the benefit from these encounters. The topics, when chosen by visiting or host adults, should be those in which they are themselves interested so that they may be able to communicate this interest to the children. If the topic chosen does have even a tenuous relationship with the curriculum or with some forthcoming examination, this is likely to be regarded as a bonus, but it is less important than the qualities of a stimulating speaker or mentor. Mechanical aids or even samples can add to the occasion, but the most vital part is the interchange of ideas between the adult and the children. An adult can often learn from such children.

Whether the gifted children are being taken by the teacher or by another adult, the level of the content and the vocabulary used must be high enough to challenge them. In the case of the adult from outside the school, it is probable that the material or content will be used normally with adults: attempts to lower it to the assumed level of the audience of children may lead to a patronizing approach which will, in turn, lead to disappointment and boredom. The vocabulary need not be watered down, provided that the children are encouraged to ask for an explanation of any word or technical term which they may not understand, and which is necessary for a full appreciation of the talk or demonstration. This arrangement does not remove the need for the teacher or other adult to check from time to time that the children are following and understanding. Gifted children, like all other children, are soon lost to a teacher or speaker who allows his stimulation to wane during a lesson. Another teaching principle that is worth remembering is that there are advantages in linking the topic with the known interests of the children. Nevertheless it is true to say that where children encounter a gifted adult it is remarkable how wide the interests of the children seem to be.

A technique of presentation which seems to work well with gifted children is that of making the familiar seem unfamiliar, which is, after all, the basis of many of the most valuable inventions ever made. Not only in the exercise in which the pupils were encouraged to think of teachers as learners and children as teachers (see pages 136–7), but also in discussions, the children would remark, "I did not see it that way before." One feels that a remark of this kind whould always be followed up with an invitation to the youngsters to try to look at other familiar occurrences in their daily lives or in their thoughts in an equally unusual way. If Kafka's

The Metamorphosis seems too strong a stimulus for young children, then *Alice in Wonderland* might serve instead.

A further suggestion is that more time should be taken by parents, Head teachers, class teachers (and, indeed, other adults, such as leaders of uniformed and youth organizations) to explain their aims. Parents might well explain to their offspring what they are attempting to do in the running of the household, or even their choice of a school. The Head teacher of a school might explain to at least some of the older pupils something of the organization of the school and the reasons for certain decisions and arrangements. This explanation should be at the level of the children rather than that of the Parent—Teachers' meeting. In the classroom, the teacher can explain, even in a primary school, what he is trying to do and why he has made certain groupings. At the secondary level, aims should be explained clearly in the hope that examinations will be shown in their proper perspective and that pupils and teachers may be able to co-operate more fully.

Finally, there is a need for teachers of gifted children to rethink some of their ideas and preconceptions. Sometimes, teachers seem to be over-protective of children, maintaining that this or that activity is beyond the physical or mental capacity of their pupils. In some instances the teacher may be better equipped to judge the physical capacity than the mental. This protectiveness is sometimes shown in the excessive simplification of vocabulary or of ideas, thus rendering much of the school-work of little value to the gifted. Where bright children are concerned, teachers would do well to raise their own level of aspiration so that they too might work, for a little time at least, at a higher level than circumstances normally allow. Those teachers who tend to be too diffident about their own abilities in relation to gifted children should try to welcome the opportunities offered by the appearance of one or two gifted children in their class. Perhaps the best cure for such diffidence on the part of an intelligent adult is to take a course on the education of gifted children, and then to undertake some actual teaching of a few such children. He will probably find that he is kept much too busy to be aware of any of his former diffidence, and, while emerging from the experience sadder and wiser, may soon be tempted to repeat the experience. He will soon join the ranks of

those who look forward to their next meeting with the group of
gifted children, and who emerge from each encounter exhilarated
but conscious that "much virtue has gone out of them."

Selective Bibliography

Beck, J., *How to Raise a Brighter Child* (Trident Press, USA, 1967)

Branch, M., & Cash, A., *Gifted Children* (London, Souvenir Press, 1966)

Bridges, S. A. (Ed.), *Gifted Children and the Brentwood Experiment* (London, Pitman, 1969)

Bridges, S. A., *I. Q. 150* (London, Priory Press, 1973)

Burt, C., "The Gifted Child" (*British Journal of Statistical Psychology*, Vol. XIV, Part 2 1961)

Burt, C., "The Gifted Child" (*Year Book of Education*, Evans, 1962)

Davie, R., Butler, N., & Goldstein, H., *From Birth to Seven. Studies in Child Development* (Longmans, 1972)

Dunn, L. M., *Exceptional Children in School* (New York, Holt, Rinehart & Winston, Ltd, 1965)

Durr, W. K., *The Gifted Student* (New York, Oxford University Press, 1964)

Fliegler, L. A. (Ed.), *Curriculum Planning for the Gifted* (Englewood Cliffs, N. J., Prentice-Hall, 1961)

Gallagher, J. J., *Teaching the Gifted Child* (Boston, Allyn & Bacon Inc., 1964)

Getzels, J. W., & Jackson, B. W., *Creativity and Intelligence* (New York, J. Wiley & Sons, 1962)

Goertzel, V., & Goertzel, M. G., *Cradles of Eminence* (Boston, Little, Brown & Co., 1962)

Gowan, J. C., *Development of the Creative Individual* (San Diego, Robert Knapp, 1971)

Gowan, J. C., & Demos, G. D., *The Education and the Guidance of the Ablest* (Illinois, C. C. Thomas, 1964)

Guilford, J. P., *Intellective Factors in Productive Thinking* (University of Southern California, 1963)

Guilford, J. P., *Personality* (McGraw-Hill, 1959)

Guilford, J. P., *Intelligence, Creativity and their Educational Implications* (San Diego, Robert Knapp, 1968)

Hildreth, G. H., *Introduction to the Gifted* (McGraw-Hill, 1966)

Hollingworth, L. S., *Children Above 180 I.Q.* (New York, World Book Co., 1942)

Hudson, L., *Contrary Imaginations* (London, Pelican, 1967)

Hudson, L., *Frames of Mind* (London, Pelican, 1968)

Inhelder, B., & Piaget, J., *The Early Growth of Logic in the Child* (London, Routledge and Kegan Paul, 1964)

Kellmer-Pringle, A., *Able Misfits* (Longmans, 1969)

Kogan, N., & Wallach, M. A., *Modes of Thinking in Young Children* (New York, Holt, Rinehart & Winston, Ltd, 1965)

Lowenfield V., & Brittain, W. L., *Creative and Mental Growth* (London, Macmillan, 1966)

Ogilvie, E., *Gifted Children in Primary Schools* (London, Macmillan, 1973)

Osborn, C. F., *Applied Imagination* (New York, Scribner & Sons, 1957)

Piaget, J., *The Origins of Intelligence in the Child* (London, Routledge and Kegan Paul, 1953)

Serebriakoff, V., *A Mensa Analysis and History* (Hutchinson, 1966)

Shields, J. B., *The Gifted Child* (National Foundation for Educational Research, 1968)

Tannenbaum, A. J., *Adolescents' Attitudes towards Academic Brilliance* (Teachers' College, Columbia University, 1965)

Taylor, C. W., *Creativity: Progress and Potential* (New York, McGraw-Hill, 1964)

Taylor, C. W., *Widening Horizons in Creativity* (New York, J. Wiley & Sons, 1964)

Terman, L. M., *et al.*, *Genetic Studies of Genius* (Stanford University Press: Vol. 1, 1925; Vol. 2, 1926; Vol. 3, 1930; Vol. 4, 1947; Vol. 5, 1959)

Torrance, E. P., *Guiding Creative Talent* (Englewood Cliffs, N.J., Prentice-Hall, 1962)

Torrance, E. P., *Education and the Creative Potential* (University of Minnesota Press, 1963)

Torrance, E. P., *Rewarding Creative Behaviour* (Englewood Cliffs, N.J., Prentice-Hall, 1965)

Torrance, E. P., *Encouraging Creativity in the Classroom* (Dubuque, W. C. Brown, 1970)

Torrance, E. P., & Myers, R. E., *Creativity, Learning and Teaching* (New York, Dodd, Mead Co., 1970)

Vernon, P. E., "Creativity and Intelligence" (*Educational Research* Vol. VI, No. 3, 1964)

Waddington, M., "Problems of Educating Gifted Children with special reference to Britain" (*Year Book of Education*, Evans) 1961

Wall, W. D., "Highly Intelligent Children, Part 1. The Psychology of the Gifted; Part 2. The Education of the Gifted" (*Educational Research*, Vol. II, No. 2, 1960)

PUBLICATION AWAITED

The Report and some of the Materials used by N. Tempest on the University of Liverpool Experiment at Southport

Index